SPRING CREEK

BOOKS BY NICK LYONS

SPRING CREEK

Nick Lyons

Drawings by Mari Lyons

THE ATLANTIC MONTHLY PRESS

NOTE ON THE DRAWINGS

The drawings in this book were not specifically prepared as illustra-
tions for *Spring Creek* but were made, "on location," with different
pens and pencils, in various notebooks, over a period of several
years. They were selected from several hundred such drawings for
use in the book.

Sections of this book originally appeared, in very different form, in several periodicals,
chiefly *Fly Fisherman* magazine. I did not include them, intact, in my last book—a
collection of "Seasonable Angler" columns—because I think I always knew that I would
someday write a book about Spring Creek and would want to change, expand, and
adapt those columns for what would have to be a book of its own, with a life of its
own. My thanks to *Fly Fisherman* for publishing those first versions of these chapters,
and to *Fly Fishing Quarterly* and *Field & Stream* for paragraphs and phrases I've plucked
from articles I wrote for them, which now have new homes. And my special thanks to
Carl Navarre for his thoughtful suggestions and to Bonnie Levy for her wise editing.

Published simultaneously in Canada
Printed in the United States of America

Library of Congress Cataloging-in-Publication Data

Lyons, Nick.
    Spring Creek / Nick Lyons; drawings by Mari Lyons.
    ISBN 0-87113-525-6
    1. Fly fishing. 2. Fishing. I. Title.
  SH456.L97   1992   799.1'755—dc20   92-13026

Design by Liz Driesbach

THE ATLANTIC MONTHLY PRESS
19 Union Square West
New York, NY 10003

First printing

CONTENTS

FOR

H. G. Wellington

WITH GREAT AFFECTION

1

Mornings

Every morning around ten, for thirty-one days, we'd stash our gear in the huge tan Suburban and head for the river. We'd head up the first hill, onto the highest bench, then rattle along the single rutted lane across the fields of wheatgrasses spotted with dark-green weed and sweet clover and pale-yellow prickly pear. There were always clusters of antelope in the fields. Often they would watch us—inert, wary, turning slightly so as always to be facing the car— until we came close enough to be a threat, though we were no threat. Often there were several spindly legged fawns with them, born several weeks earlier; Herb had seen a doe drop one in the narrow

4   road and he had stopped and watched and then gone around them. "Not enough meat to make a decent sandwich," he once said in his deep voice—the words always curt, final—watching a newborn antelope scamper away, already quick and lithe. Overhead, curlews with long curved beaks canted away, shrieking, and often we saw their chicks, which had no beaks yet, scuttling from us into the grasses.

Every morning, at the bluff that ended the last bench, we would stop the car and get out, and then look down into the valley, stretching off in front of us as far as we could see, with several braids of the river meandering through it like a blue ribbon stretched out casually upon a great green and tan rug. Except for the willows on the inner rim of the bench, near the headwaters of the East Branch, and the ragged line of cottonwoods in the distance, there were no trees: the river lay open and exposed and I knew at once that it would be hard to fish, with no cover, no breaks from the sun, with every movement of rod or line or person taken to be one of the trout's great predators here—pelican, osprey, kingfisher, merganser, heron, gull. An anthropologist who visited compared it to the Serengeti Plain, and it has that same broad fertile space.

We'd have the whole day, from then until dark, to fish the river. We could fish it anywhere we chose—miles and miles of it. We could fish it as hard or in as leisurely a manner as suited our fancy. We could go back to the ranch for lunch, or pack in a sandwich or some elk sticks, or fish straight through, hard, intently. Sometimes Pat, Herb's wife, and Mari would bring down lunch in the other Suburban.

I soon realized that Spring Creek was the most interesting river I had ever fished or could imagine; and I learned that it was loaded with secrets that would take exceptional skill to learn. At first I felt very privileged to be fishing the river, but soon my thoughts turned chiefly to where we'd fish and what the fishing would be like and when it would come and what fishing we'd already had. Within a week, the days blurred and I had to concentrate to separate them, keep them in sequence, though I have had no trouble finding in my brain the full and vivid picture of a hundred moments, most of the fish I raised for the month I was there. Those were halcyon days and they changed my fly-fishing life forever.

From the top of the last bench the river looked blue, though up close it was green and blue and a dozen variants of amber, umber, coral, and beige; it was really colorless as water in a glass, pure spring water, but it took on the hues of its bottom and of the banks. Sometimes the crystalline water was slow and moody or flat; then there were the fifty or so great bends of the West Branch, some tight, some broad as avenues; there were riffles and chops and pools and tails and swampy runs and brisk runs and shallow flats a couple of hundred feet across, all in dozens of configurations, so that there were thousands of different fishing chances. Everywhere, the water was the clearest I'd ever seen, water in which the auburn, spotted forms of the trout and the wavering, hairlike masses of elodea and watercress were ghostlike. The river held trout large enough to make my eyes pop—mostly browns, all wild, with a scattering of rainbows—which would rise to flies the size of gnats. Nursed on the muddy, milky waters of the Croton watershed near New York City, where I had fished with worms and spinning lures, it all spooked me silly. The river seemed quite beyond the meager talents I thought I could bring to it.

When the wind did not ruffle the surface of the river too harshly—giving it a slate, opaque cover—the water was so translucent that you could see distinctly to the bottom of the deepest pools. What I could see in some of them, five to eight feet down, wavering like living shadows near the bottom, sent shock waves through me.

We would stop at the final bluff to look for the blue herons, which pecked holes in even very large trout and killed many smaller fish.

6   They were astonishing hunters and several times I saw one result of their efforts: a beautiful, wild brown trout with a hole right on the top of its back, as if someone had shoved a pencil down an inch or so, very hard. Herb did not like them. "They can't even pick up some of the larger trout they stick," he said. After I'd seen three with that raw pencil hole in their backs, I felt the same, let the Audubon Society be damned. If there was a heron hunting, it would usually whirl into flight, its gigantic wings flapping heavily, merely at our appearance more than several hundred yards away. I never saw one until it was in flight, and at first mistook the six or seven pairs of sandhill cranes that nested in the valley for herons—though the sandhills traveled in pairs, the herons always alone.

We'd look for several minutes from the bluff, standing quite still and sometimes shivering from the early cold, and begin to think about the day and the weather and the flies and what had happened the day before and which section of Spring Creek we'd fish that day. Then we'd head down the last hill.

Now there was nothing to think about but the fishing. It was a truly remarkable river, but on a given day you could catch nothing; during the weeks I was there, three people—all fine fishermen—got skunked. Once I got none; Herb always got fish. Flies might hatch upriver but not down. The sun might be too bright, the wind too strong, relentless. The large pool on the East Branch might explode with feeding fish or remain perfectly placid, as if it did not contain a trout. The Two Islands Pool might go berserk. The Great Horseshoe Bend—as distinguished from many lesser Horseshoe Bends—might look barren, or might have one, three, or thirty fish rising. But once I had looked into several of the deepest pools I knew something of what the river contained, everywhere, and a shiver of expectation ran through me every time I looked at the water, anywhere, or pitched a fly into it, and still does even now, years later, whenever I think of Spring Creek.

In the deep pools, when the light was just right, you could see fifty or sixty wild browns, of all sizes—a few ten-inchers, a whole slew of fish between fifteen and nineteen inches, and a few old alligators that would go twenty-five or more. Sometimes, concentrating on some deeply undercut bank, if you were lucky, you could catch a glimpse of something dark and larger than anything your imagination could conjure. Was thirty-two or thirty-four inches an exaggeration? I don't think so. Several times, fishing carelessly up the West Branch, I'd spook one of those old fellows and it would bolt from a dark bank—black and too slow for a trout, as if it really wasn't afraid of me or anything else in this world, though prudence dictated it move: a fish the size of a muskrat or a dog, coming right past me, black and thick, scaring me half out of my boots.

But Spring Creek was also a place where solitude and quiet camaraderie were possible. It might be a river crammed with wild trout of great average size and great wariness, a place where I had more interesting fishing chances than I could imagine having anywhere else, but it was also a place where I made some great friends and learned more than I can tell.

At the bottom of the hill there was a shallow stretch of the river that the Suburban could ford easily. But usually before we crossed we made a short trip downstream to the right and the Suburban leaned down toward the river and I leaned over Herb's shoulder to see the water. On the way back to the crossing, with the vehicle dipping low on my side now, I had an unobstructed view of the river. The water was thin here—perhaps a foot to eighteen inches deep, over a sandy bottom, spotted with waterweed. Darting across the bottom, their shadows more palpable than their bodies, were a couple dozen trout. They were long and tan—some darker than others—and from the car we never saw them at rest. They were elusive, evanescent; they seemed born paranoids, afraid of every motion, every shadow. I

8   hadn't the faintest idea how to approach them, or how to catch such
fish, but they were beautiful to watch in their wildness, and they were
very large—some twenty-two inches or more—and they gave to
each morning a kind of benediction. And they always roused my
metabolism. I called this the Paranoid Pool and, from the beginning,
I never expected to catch a fish in it, though Herb said there were
times, when there was a slight chop on the water perhaps, when the
fish could be caught, when you might gain entrance to the Castle. As
day after day passed, I grew more and more determined to be skillful
enough to catch one of these fish, fish as tough to catch as any I have
ever seen. By the third week I had found half a dozen such spots on
the river, many of them even more difficult to fish.

Below the Paranoid Pool there was a huge shallow flat, several
hundred feet across and twice as long, and then the water narrowed,
rushed against the far bank, split off into a back channel and disappeared, and the main current formed an exquisite run of several
hundred yards that emptied into a broad right-angle bend as the back
channel joined the main flow below the island. This was a deep pool,
braided with a farrago of currents; it held a great head of trout and
you could usually take a fish or two here, whatever the circumstances,
but it was very hard to fish wisely and consistently well.

After we'd looked at the Farrago Pool we'd head back, then ford
the river and rumble slowly up the rutted and pitted dirt track that
skirted the dozens of S curves of the West Branch, looking for flies or
rises, flushing more curlew and their chicks, as well as little killdeer
that hugged the road and then disappeared into the grasses, spotting
a white-tailed deer or a cluster of sandhill cranes beyond the fence that
kept the cattle from trampling the banks of the river. In places you
could see where an oxbow had silted in, grown grass, and caused the
river to adjust its path. The older routes were a delicate, lighter,
fresher green than the other grasses. Herb had been advised to tinker
with the river, to add structures that would help prevent the silting

of bends, but his principle of conservation was abrupt and final: Leave it alone. He believed that the river would change, shift, adjust, suffer, flourish, and take quite good care of itself, thank you. Fencing out the cattle was an exception. And once he and I, on a scorching July afternoon, planted about a hundred willow shoots—none of which survived.

As we drove slowly down the West Branch, we'd hear the ice in the lemonade jug rattle, and we'd keep an eye peeled to the river. We'd always pass the decaying carcass of a calf struck by lightning that spring, and I'd always look to see if it was less of itself. The interior had collapsed and the skin kept getting tighter. At first there was an eager mass of insects everywhere on it, but as the season progressed the carcass kept shrinking, as if by itself, as if it was struggling to get gone from this place. The carcass always made me think of Richard Eberhart's poem "The Groundhog," where that little creature keeps decaying until, near the end, the poet sees merely the beautiful architecture of its bones and then, at the very end, when there is less than a spot, thinks of Alexander in his tent and Saint Theresa in her wild lament, and about mortality and such large matters. The calf carcass didn't vanish that summer; it was too tough. But it decreased. I tried to find some metaphor in it but decided to let it remain simply a decaying calf's carcass, several yards east of a run that led to one of the best back bends on the West Branch.

In fifteen minutes we'd be at the south end of the property, opposite a huge bend pool that pinched into a slick that you could watch comfortably from the warm car while the world warmed. We rarely saw fish move on our early trip upriver, though we often paused at several of the larger bends for a moment or two. At the south end we had an unobstructed view of a lovely run; its glassy surface and slight gradient let us see instantly the slightest bulge on the surface.

Herb usually saw signs of fish first.

He'd point and I'd have to look closely and then I'd see a dorsal slightly breaking the surface, or bending reeds near the far point, or a wake, or the delicate spreading flower of a sipping rise, or a quick black head, up then down.

Herb and I had exchanged hundreds of letters—often several a week—in the years before I first fished Spring Creek with him. Though he did not tie, his observations on fly design, the attitude of flies on the water, knots, new gadgets, leaders, fly-rod length and design and action, technological improvements of various kinds, books old and new, and dozens of other fly-fishing subjects were acute and frank. He fished only with the dry fly and his observations were directed exclusively to matters connected to a fly that floats—but the word "purist" would sound silly if I used it to describe anything about him. He had more fun fishing the dry fly; he conceded the rest of the river to the trout; he enjoyed that visual connection to his quarry— the link that occurs where our world of air meets theirs, on the surface. He could be growly on the subject, claiming that he was a "fly" fisherman, not an "artificial bait" fisherman, but the heart of the matter was less philosophy than hedonism, I think: he enjoyed the one more than the other.

He had clearly read far more than I ever will about fly fishing and he read with a shrewd and independent mind, guffawing at pretenders and second-handers and people who didn't give credit and "light-weights" (a favorite term of his), even if I had published or edited or introduced such people. An English friend—the author of half a dozen books on fly fishing—said: "He has a wonderfully grumpy, bollocking exterior which hides a man of great kindness. He is also a remarkable fly fisherman and makes me feel like a novice." I did not know when I flew out to be with him whether he was the superb fly fisher the Englishman and others said he was, but his opinions were sharp, often raw, always telling, even when they made me smart. What he did he insisted upon doing deftly. He spoke abruptly, sometimes in half sentences, often with laconic wit, in a low baritone. He scared the socks off at least one mutual friend. Thinking back, these many years later, I realize that mingled with the special expectation you feel when you sense you are about to begin the new and unknown was the nagging sense that we were from wildly different worlds, that up close the visit would prove a disaster.

I came full of expectation and some trepidation, and then, as early as that first morning, I forgot what I had expected and whatever it was I might have feared, and thought only of the water before us and the discrete possibilities of the day. The days were crammed with surprises anyway, of the kind that any great river provides, and I could not have imagined what happened any more than I have the imagination to invent a river like Spring Creek. For years it has so dominated my thoughts that I have been able to think and write of practically nothing else. Setting out to write this book has become as much an exorcism as a report, a private rage for order, for clarity. I want very much to see that period clearly, from mornings to evenings, from knowing nothing to knowing something, in all its tension, intensity, challenge, and fun, from when I met the river in late June to when I left it in the bright sun of late July.

In the mornings, when the grasses were still wet with a bright silver sheen and the antelope fled and the curlew flew ahead of us as we rattled along the rutted and pitted track across the benches down to the river, we always felt the nervous tingling of expectation.

At first I wanted to fish all of the river at once, and I felt anxious when we chose one spot. The fishing might be better upriver or down, I thought. It made me uneasy. But after a few days I settled down, took matters one at a time and carefully, and felt content as we

reconnoitered downstream, past Paranoid Pool and the big flat and Farrago Pool, then looked at the first few pools on the East Branch, and then drove slowly up the length of the West Branch, noting the carcass and the old oxbows, pausing at four or five bends.

Few flies would hatch until 10:15 or a bit later, depending upon the temperature, and we'd sit and talk quietly in the big tan Suburban, about books or fishing or the condition of the water, or not talk, and then we'd see some flies on the front window. They might be small dark caddis or the first Pale Morning Duns, delicate and faintly yellow. Herb would point and mumble and I'd give a little electric exclamation. Then a fish would show.

Was it a one-riser?

Yes, one rise, then gone.

"Not exactly a feeding frenzy," Herb might say.

But then there was another. And another. It was starting. We'd both make guttural sounds and not voice the obvious. One of us would point.

"Better get your rod down," Herb would say, and I'd say that he should get his down. In a few more moments one of us, usually me, would get out of the car ever so slowly, never taking eyes from the river, unsnap the rod from the carrier on the car roof, select and tie on a fly, and prepare to fish.

In the mornings we always looked and talked first. Then the sun grew warmer and before too long we would find some fish working. The river was merely what a river ought to be—varied, fecund, wild, with large trout, skittery as hummingbirds, that pretty much liked a fly to look pretty much like the thing it was eating—and as I looked from the Suburban and then went out to meet it I always felt that the world and I were moments from being born.

2

Easy Chances

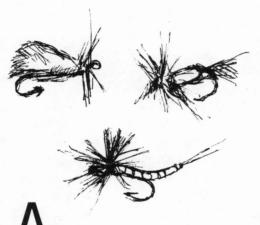

At the south end of the property, three miles up from where we crossed, there were two pools: the one where we usually sat, waiting for the first flies—the slick with very thin water that was tremendously difficult—and the other that, when you learned it, was a pushover. We often sat at the South End Pool first, waiting to begin the day; but it was a humbling pool, unlike the other, a hundred yards downstream. Herb called the easy pool The Nursery.

The day I arrived, hours after the plane touched down, Herb positioned me in the South End Pool and I promptly put down a half dozen slurping trout. Then he walked me down to The Nursery.

Here the water rushes down a shallow, dipping gradient, makes a ninety-degree turn, scoots along the far bank where it builds a foam-flecked eddy, narrows and speeds up, then runs for fifty yards in a canal-stretch in which I've never done well. You fish it from the inside of the bend, over a slack silt bed. The fish are in one of three or four current lanes, which begin fifteen feet from the near bank and run over to the foam line along the far bank, sixty feet across the river. The water comes down sharply from the shallow run and breaks over a ridge, below which is a deep pool. The place is a food factory; the few fish we killed that came from The Nursery were stuffed with riffle beetle larvae, water worms, and a variety of nymphs.

The center current is tangled and fast, so the key to the pool is always how you mend your line. You fish the near current first, either at the head of the pool or in the belly of it, where the currents come together, rush against the downstream end of the bend, and circle downstream. Because of the clip at which the water travels, the fish come—either to naturals or imitations—with a splash or spurt rise. The chop to the surface shields the fisherman and you can be quite close to a fish without frightening it; the chop always helps you to float the fly a good distance, too. Days after I arrived, when the Green Drakes were hatching at midday, The Nursery was peppered with these spurts of water, like bluefish into a school of spearing or bunker.

That first day I looked at The Nursery and saw twenty places to fish—and none. I fussed with my fly boxes and took out a #12 Hairwing Coachman, which I thought I could see in such heavy water.

"You'll do better with a number fourteen Humpy," Herb said.

I switched, tied the fly on quickly, and false cast a dozen or so times to bring enough line beyond the tip. I'd focused on a fetching current three-quarters of the way across-river and started lengthening the line to reach it.

"Shorter," said Herb.

I cast twice, much shorter than I'd wanted; the fly hit the surface and jerked downstream and dragged in seconds. Next time I tried to mend the line on the water and barely got another few inches of float. It was going to be a disaster.

"Hook the line upstream when you cast—before the fly hits the water," Herb advised, and when I did, putting a large loop of line above the fly, I got a better float; and when I snaked the line a little, as I worked farther across the pool, into the greater tangles of currents, I did even better. It was a simple enough adjustment and I felt sure I'd take a fish now, but none rose.

I asked Herb to show me the drill. He waited ten minutes, talked to me about fishing the closer areas more carefully and the absolute need not to false cast so much, and then tied on a #16 Goddard Caddis. He false cast once, away from the water he was going to fish, and then cast to the head of the nearest current. The fly floated pertly and high—and on the third cast there was a quick spurt rise and he had on a substantial fish that led him around the corner, downstream; he followed it for thirty-five yards, held his ground, brought it in, and released the fish a few moments later, without benefit of net. He didn't like nets and discouraged his guests from using them. "Tangle in the gills," he said. "And they aren't necessary, are they?"

His fish, the first brown trout I'd seen from Spring Creek, was brilliantly orange and brightly spotted—a Tiepolo of a trout, with a bullet head and broad confirmation, a wild, firm, miraculous creature. It was eighteen or nineteen inches long, perhaps two and a half pounds. When Herb called it a "nice little fish" my knees took on a slight, uncontrollable shake.

I knew some things but not enough. Spring Creek was a special river and it required new, better skills.

Herb taught me to mend in the air sharply, to match the speed and heaviness of the current; once the line hit the water in such a turbulent pool, it was too late. He talked to me about flies, and it was clear that he preferred those that imitated an insect, not Coachmen or Humpys or other attractors. He talked to me about size and conformation, and how different kinds of water on Spring Creek demanded different styles of tying as well as different patterns.

I felt I knew nothing, that all my years of fussing around trout rivers had been with the aimless curiosity of a dog.

I had always been able to take trout. From the first trout I caught, by gigging it in high summer on a long Carlisle hook strapped to a willow branch, when I was six, I had decent instincts for the hunt. I had become a deadly worm fisherman in my early teens, using a very long, very heavy collapsible steel fly rod; I never used flies, which I knew would not work. By lob or by dangle, with live minnows, caterpillars, grasshoppers, as well as worms, I got good enough to take serious numbers of trout from the heavily fished watershed rivers within sixty miles of New York City. A teenager with a minnow or a worm and some talent is a serious threat to such rivers, even a menace, and should be outlawed. But then, in my midteens, I saw a fellow my age take six or seven trout—just like that—on a spinning rod, with a lure called the Homa-Reverso—and that became my weapon until my early twenties. During my spinning years I was even more of a menace than any kid with a minnow, and should have been outlawed.

I'm not quite sure why one switches from spinning to fly fishing—it's like going from something that works to something that, for a long time, doesn't work. If it ain't broke, why fix it?

Fly fishing seemed not to work at all at first, and I resisted it. But that gorgeous, speckled creature—so mysterious and shy—more and more seemed *made* for fly fishing. It ate flies, which appeared mysteriously on the water and had a secret life beneath the surface; its rise was delicate and haunting. Often you fished for a trout you saw and had hunted rather than simply casting a lure into a likely spot. I felt so proud of that first trout I caught on a fly that I wanted more, right away—as much of it as I could get.

It may be difficult to tell *why* one switches, but the picture of how—in all its delicious particulars—is familiar enough. One cannot get enough equipment: seven rods are not enough; three thousand flies do not quite serve all possible contingencies. One cannot study entomology hard enough, read enough magazines and books. Marketers of such stuff call this an "information-intensive" period; I think the novice is just gut-hooked and loony. There's so much to learn: plop casts and reach casts, subtler stream reading, twenty-seven different knots, wading techniques, insect cycles, ninety-three new fly patterns "you can't do without," new hot spots, new techniques . . . of which there are as many as rocks in a stream. By comparison, spinning is one-dimensional: it bypasses virtually all that makes fly fishing a joy and a consummate challenge, and it leaps solely to the catching of trout, which it does very well, but with a limited number of necessary options (I last used a C. P. Swing exclusively and never failed to catch good fish).

When I became addicted to fly fishing, in my early twenties, I stopped spinning altogether. I think I had the feeling then that it was unfair—not only to the trout but to my passion.

Fly fishing is both a restriction (like putting up a net and outlining a court, so two tennis players don't just smash a ball at each other, wantonly) and an opener of new worlds. Nymph, streamer, wet fly, dry fly? Which, in which pattern, will work best at a given time?

At first you want to catch *any* fish with a fly; then you want to catch a lot of fish—I've heard hundreds of fly fishermen in this stage boast of sixty- or seventy-fish days; and then you want especially big fish. There's a famous maxim to this effect; I surely have lived it.

I can remember, with a bright blush of embarrassment, a night out

West, hitting a perfect hurricane of a trout binge; they were feeding with abandon and were as *un*selective as bluefish. I tried to catch every one of them. I fished hard and brought the fish in as fast as I dared and then quickly cast again. I'd have won tournaments. I might have broken records. I couldn't get enough of it. After all the years of catching so few, often so arbitrarily, it seemed, I'd finally hit them just right and I wasn't going to walk away from it. And I didn't—not until all light was gone and rain began to pelt me, and even then I wondered whether the pock marks on the river were *all* from rain or whether a few good fish weren't still working.

In the process of learning to catch a lot of fish, you are fascinated, at turns, with ingenious nymphing techniques, the possibilities of lead-core or shooting-head or sink-tip lines, the fish-killing qualities of the Zonker or the Bitch Creek Special or the Leech or the Gold Brassie or the Gray Fox Variant; you learn the names of more bugs than you'd encounter in a lifetime; you learn to cast into the wind and how to hook your line to the left or right. You want to become eminently versatile, able to meet any fishing situation, even lethal. You want to be able to catch any fish under any circumstances. If the fish are deep, you want to know it and go there with your fly; if they're taking chironomids in the film, you want to have the right imitation and fish there; if the water is high, you want to be able to take trout any way you can, on heavily weighted nymphs or some dazzling new streamer that uses half of a rabbit's back strapped on the hook. You want to learn it all—but mostly you want to succeed every time.

But if you fish often enough for trout and hard enough, and if you read enough of the words of the experts, finally you get a little better—and after a couple dozen fine and successful days of it, you may, like I did, look around you one afternoon and say, "There's something more here—and I want it."

What I wanted were harder trout.

Now one may *make* a trout harder by adding more limitations; think of how much harder—though not necessarily better, or more interesting—tennis would be if the net was raised a couple of feet. In fly fishing, you can restrict your "weapons"—perhaps to a floating line or a floating fly or to a #1 bamboo rod made exclusively by a particular Tibetan monk, fished exclusively while standing on one's head. Fortunately, trout are hard enough and make us ludicrous easily enough without our resorting to all such tricks; Mozart's music is enough of a miracle for me without the movie trying to tell us that genius is the ability to play that way upside down and backward . . . while giggling.

I had wanted more of a challenge and had looked around me; but I did not know what I was looking for until I came to Spring Creek.

The Nursery was only a primitive form of Spring Creek fishing but it was an excellent place for me to begin to learn, for it was crammed with big fish and at least some of them were generous to a fault, forgiving, and anxious to rise even when there were no flies on the water. Fishing it on and off those first few days, I began to see when I had lined an area by aggressively trying a longer cast before one was needed; I watched when and figured out why my fly dragged and tried to apply what Herb had told me. Since I hooked four or five fish and even caught one or two, Herb had a chance to tell me about playing fish; he insisted I fight them with more authority. I played them too hard and lost them or too gingerly and let them take me several hundred yards downstream. Several times, petrified by a large fish, I played it by holding line in my left hand—and failed; and I resolved always, without exception to get a fish on the reel and keep it there for an entire fight whenever I could. Catching a lot of fish, and big fish, gives you a chance to develop such skills.

More and more, I began to watch every movement Herb made

with his fly rod—often including little adjustments of hand that I'd never seen before, that I could not at first duplicate.

On those first mornings, we'd generally look at the South End Pool first, I'd spoil it, and then we'd drop down to The Nursery, where I'd take a few fish, raise a good many others, and then we'd drive to one of the larger bends on the West Branch. I might take a couple of fish in The Nursery, another at the Great Horseshoe Bend, two from a couple of honey holes Herb knew, and lose five or six. None of the pools had names, but Herb would refer to the South End Pool and the Pond and the Horseshoe Bend and a couple of others and I gradually took some of his names and added a few of my own, like Paranoid.

When we'd fished the West Branch for a couple of hours, we'd drop further downstream to the lower sections. There, often around midday, we'd find some feeding fish and make our stand. Here the fishing was tougher. The water was flatter, there were fewer undercut banks, and the fish could only be fished to when they were feeding, when you had a target to guide you. If you cast blindly, you spoiled the water—and sometimes were not ready to cast when fish did rise. Leaders had to be a notch finer, flies smaller, casting much more precise.

Just when I'd had a couple of five- or six-fish mornings—with browns from seventeen to nineteen inches—and was tickled pink with myself, I felt hopeless again. At first I'd cast boldly and all five feeding fish would go down the first time the line went over them. I'd false cast five or six times and that would scare a whole pod of rising fish. I'd stand or crouch too high and the fish would flee from my silhouette.

Herb barked at me for false casting so much and I began to accelerate my casts with more power on the second or third movement of the rod, and I kept all line in the air away from the fish for as long as possible. I was amazed at how Herb could cast seventy feet or so with only one false cast—and the line came low to the water and never over the fish. Several times when I was after a good fish, I'd hear him grumble, "Lined him." A couple of friends later told me they were paralyzed when he watched them fish. I simply never felt that way—though I hate most people to watch me and have had my greatest disasters when they did. Perhaps it was that from the beginning I viewed Herb as having special knowledge, of a virtually unique stripe, about this river and about fly fishing, and I never failed to learn from his tough eye—and deep voice.

And I kept learning immensely from watching him fish. I could see that he cast one-tenth as much as I did and never when he did not see a fish rise. Clearly he liked this flat-water fishing best; just as clearly, it was the fishing I did least well at.

There were fewer rising fish in some of the West Branch bends, but I did much better in them. It took little time to learn to chuck a Parachute Adams tight in against the deeply undercut banks here, in the foam line no more than inches out. Accuracy was important—but it was a primitive sort, rarely requiring either the precision or the delicacy that the flat water did. You had three or four inches on either side of the foam line usually: too far out and you'd miss catching the eye of the fish altogether, too close and you'd snag in the overhanging roots and grasses. Sometimes it was tighter than that, but it was a kind of fishing that played to my strength of knowing where fish are, and from the first days I took fish here.

One of my problems was controlling a cast. The fish in the West Branch bends were forgiving. If you didn't raise one right away, you might well raise one on your fourth or fifth cast. If I was not sufficiently accurate at first, I could be sufficiently accurate later.

On our third day out Herb asked to see my rod and pronounced it too soft. He waved my Dennis Bailey parabolic bamboo, a great favorite, a few times, looked at those intermediate windings I loved so much, and shook his head. "It's no good, Nick. It won't cast accurately; it's got no backbone."

I'd always felt the opposite: softer rod, greater delicacy. And I especially liked this rod, which had been made especially for me by the great British rodmaker. In fact, it had a story connected to it that I thought of every time I fished the rod. Dennis had hired a young, very attractive woman to do the many intermediate windings and, standing behind her, had taught her how to do so on my rod. The training took nearly a week and at the end of it the local postman, who had been observing the activity through the front window, said in a harsh Calvinist tone, "Mr. Bailey, what are you doing with that young woman in there?"

"Teaching her to whip a rod," said Dennis.

"You dirty old bastard," said the postman.

Herb's fly rod, an eight-foot graphite, was stiff as a telephone pole. He said it gave him more delicacy because he could control it better.

But what about playing fish with a rod that had no give, I asked him.

He showed me a leader he had devised the year before. It was an odd thing and I could not believe it would work, much less cast. He had inserted five or six inches of something called Shockgum between two sections of braided leader; the Shockgum was elastic and pulled to three times its length. *That* would surely hold bigger fish on a stiff rod, I thought, and it did. Some years later, fishing the Beaverhead with Al Troth, Herb and I both hooked fat four-pound fish that dove into snags—mine into tangled overhanging willows, his into a bird's nest of drowned branches. We rowed to each spot, hoping to save the fly, and in both cases the fish was still on—and in both cases we were using Herb's Shockgum leader.

Herb told me how when he'd first come to Spring Creek, more than twenty-five years earlier, he'd caught few of the larger fish except from the bends; he'd caught them on big Humpys or grasshoppers. The Catskill patterns he used worked only sporadically, and never on the flat water. So intriguing did he find the river and his fishing that he virtually stopped all other brands of fly fishing—for salmon, which he loved, for trout in a hundred other places he might have visited. He seemed to have fished every yard of Spring Creek, and to have thought about all the fishing problems it presented. And he had solved a lot of those problems. For years the fish in the large, flat, shallow pools had been impossible to take except on rare occasions— and these, I learned, were often the largest fish in Spring Creek, fish larger than any I had yet seen in the wild. But he had thought hard about the two chief problems: using a leader strong enough to hold the largest of these trout yet thin enough not to keep them from taking the fly; and finding shrewder fly designs to imitate the steady Pale Morning Dun hatch and all the other hatches on the flatter, most interesting water. He had learned of the new braided leader and then Shockgum, sent them to Craig Mathews to experiment with, eliminated a hinging effect that resulted from the first versions, modified Craig's leader, and finally built a leader that turned over smoothly, resisted the shock of a large fish taking and turning abruptly, and held huge fish, even with the stiff rods he used. He could go to 6X and 7X for any fish in the river—and in the flat water the small-size tippet proved critical. He had tried the lower-profile thorax, no-hackle, comparadun, and parachute designs and, by long trial and error, had found favorites that worked where the more upright, heavily hackled Catskill patterns did not.

And then when I or anyone else came, we leaped onto his back and, in merely a few days, could learn part of what he had painstakingly developed over a period of decades. We could be taken to fish and told how to fish, and if we listened we could take fish rather quickly, but we could not learn it all. Too much was beyond sight, though it was right in front of us: timed twists of hand on a cast that produced astonishing hooks and turns; jiggles of line that kept a fly dragless long enough to make you breathless; long, low, hard casts, with barely one false cast, that dropped the fly to the water like a piece of milkweed; a certain subtle positioning of oneself before the first cast, on the bank, low to the water, in some special relationship to the fish that permitted you to approach it at precisely the proper angle, which took me weeks to learn, even to understand.

What I could simply steal from him were his flies. He had studied Spring Creek all these years and had refined his fly needs to a dozen truly killing patterns and designs, not one of which I had used before on my Catskill rivers. He bought such flies by the gross, from the best tiers in the world, and he gave them to all of his guests by the handful; he bought parachutes from one, comparaduns from another, grasshoppers and Green Drakes from only special tiers, a special caddis from one tier and none of the man's other thirty patterns; he fished only the Hank of Hair tied for him with coastal deer hair by a friend. Larry Duckwall, one of the finest amateur tiers in the country, sent us six boxes of flies, especially tied for this river—four for me, two for Herb. He sent them in one big box, with our names on the ones for each of us. I left mine on the table for a day or so and when I looked at them again my name was crossed out and Herb's put in; so I crossed out his name on his boxes and put on mine—and we sort of shared flies. He had hundreds of boxes of flies, anyway, and I was encouraged to steal what I needed—which I did, sparingly.

We were getting on very well. I no longer worried that he'd make a decent sandwich of me. Some friend must have asked Herb about me on the telephone because I heard him say, "He's certifiable," which I took to be a great compliment.

* * *

Several times that first week Herb left me on the lower West Branch and drove the Suburban a quarter of a mile or more upstream, so I could fish up to it. Here the river made one S curve after the other, with fish along the far rim of the arc, under the inside point of a bend, under the banks on the near side, in the deepest heart of the pool. A few might be rising or the pool might be quiet. Because of the high banks, which shielded the water from the light, the water seemed opaque and only in a few places could you see into its depths. But next to The Nursery, this was the most fertile part of the river to fish, and later, on days when I had been frustrated by the flat-water fishing, I often found some excuse to come back to this section, which was always generous.

The first time Herb left me at the very bottom of the West Branch, where it enters the main river—the fourth or fifth day I was there—I took three huge fish on almost as many casts, from the first pool. All of them brought me back downstream to the main river. These were fish in the eighteen- to twenty-inch range and I thought I'd never get to the second pool. I was using a Parachute Adams, #16, which Herb had told me was too effective, and it proved as irresistible to the trout as a chocolate cherry to a boy. The fish were in the foam line along the far bank mostly, and I fished blind, though now and again I'd see a little spurt rise in the center current and pitch my fly there.

It was a happy business to cast thirty-five feet across the river, watch the gray fly with the white deer-hair sprout hit the foam line and begin to float downriver, and then see the splashy rise of a good brown and feel its immediate power as it went upriver, under the deeply cut banks, and then headed downstream.

With my soft bamboo rod bent in a broad arc, each fish took me back to where I had started. I don't think I progressed a hundred yards

all morning, and at the end I was muttering to myself and wondering if I'd taken eight or perhaps ten fish in no more than twice that number of casts. I've known serious fly fishermen to count each fish, note its length meticulously in a pocket notebook, give the time of day and fly used, and record each event for posterity. I can't, or won't, and don't miss the records.

When the morning was over I felt pretty cocky about myself, pretty sure I could raise any fish in the river. It wasn't so hard after all. And that cockiness didn't change when Herb put me in at a run called The Fish Trap, where the water was narrower, the smell of mint was everywhere, and you had to cast to a four-foot run along the far bank, over a bed of muck and weed that formed earlier here than on the rest of the river. The Pale Morning Duns were on that day, for the first time, and I used a little #18 thorax tie that Herb gave me that took fish regularly. These fish were also large, at least half of them eighteen inches or better, and in this charming, intimate water they inflamed my ego even more.

I was beginning to feel pretty smug about my fishing.

And that smugness grew even more when, after still more coaching, I began to take a few of the better, more difficult fish—not every one, but some.

By the sixth day I switched to one of Herb's powerful graphite rods and began to use his special leader regularly. I began to cast low and hard but to lay the fly down with much greater delicacy than I had thought ever possible for me. I made half the number of back casts I'd been making, then halved that. I fished tight in against the heavily undercut banks, in the foam line no more than a few inches out, and I began to get a foot, then four feet more of drag-free float, by hooking and ruffling the cast, adjusting it in the air and then on the water. I couldn't do everything I wanted to do all the time but my percentages were better. I stayed off the high banks altogether now and crouched and kneeled until I could barely sleep at night from the leg cramps; and then, watching Herb, I learned that sitting, though a whole lot less glamorous, was often more effective than any other position because you were so much stiller and a full few feet lower. I soon did not merely take flies from Herb but studied each one he gave me. They were no longer "pretty" but objects with form, architectonics, color, specific uses. His patterns revealed more body, floated flatter, displayed a more cunning silhouette; their color, their attitude on the water were critical. That Shockgum leader let me use 6X tippets, and thus hook and still hold the larger fish. And I began to watch more, look more sharply, fish less but more wisely.

I had come to the river full of tension and Saint Vitas's dance, but by the end of the first week, the rush, the fret, the wolf, the tooth of the world began to slip away, over the bench, past the far range of snow-capped mountain ranges, into left field. My eyes and ears began to catch more and more: the muskrat, the sparrow, the bald eagle, the white-tailed deer, the great wealth of wild things in this valley, which the two of us fished alone. But mostly I watched the water and listened to the water. Mostly I concentrated on what would improve my fishing and was anchored by that simple, practical goal. My observation became narrower and narrower, and more satisfying.

Ezra Pound, in *ABC of Reading,* tells the story of a postgraduate student, "equipped with honours and diplomas," who went to the great scientist Louis Agassiz for some "finishing touches." Agassiz showed him a small fish and asked him to describe it. The student observed that it was a sunfish. When Agassiz pressed him, the young man offered a textbook description of the creature, including its proper Latin name. Agassiz again told him to describe the fish and got a four-page essay, and then told the student really *to look* at the fish. Pound ends his anecdote: "At the end of three weeks the fish was in an advanced state of decomposition, but the student knew something about it."

Or, even wiser and more succinct, Agassiz's report: "I spent the summer traveling. I got halfway across my backyard."

And, traveling slower and slower, after a week of long mornings I had raised enough ante to play in this game; I felt I was learning *something* about Spring Creek. I could sit for a half hour like the heron—or an hour—and watch; for waiting and watching were forms of pursuit here. I could watch the flat water for the slightest sign of insect activity, any bulge or wake, the barest break of the surface.

There's one, a full fifty-five or sixty feet out. I shift my sitting position and, with only three back casts, pitch the fly a dozen feet above the feeding position of a very good brown. Not only will the fly have to land in that precise spot but it will have to land and float so that this trout will mistake it for a real Pale Morning Dun—and these Spring Creek trout are no dopes. I wouldn't move to the next table at Sam's Luncheonette or Lutèce to take a choicer salad ten feet away, I wouldn't touch even a strawberry if it moved unnaturally on the plate, and neither will this brown.

In fact, as the fly comes down over the fish, I hear the old snob say, like Mrs. Costello in *Daisy Miller*, "I would if I could, but I can't."

The wrong fly here draws sneers; drag ensures refusal; a poor cast, one that misses even the feeding rhythm of a trout, and the fly will drift over the fish a second after he's popped another peanut into his mouth.

Several casts later my fly floats merrily over the spot where the trout rose, it does not rise, my heart drops, I raise my arm to haul the line summarily off the water—"Leave it!" Herb growls; I had not thought he was watching me—the fly stops dragging, the trout turns, plugs the fly, I strike, stand up, and the big fish, my first, rockets off across the flat pool.

"A take instantaneously validates our effect," says Ted Leeson in a brilliant short essay called "On the Take," "and in so doing affords a measure of definiteness and certainty to an enterprise otherwise riddled with questions and unknowns. . . . Few things in fishing, or in life, offer this kind of satisfaction."

I don't need many of those to make a day. And then, a few days later, when the Green Drake comes, drawing splashy rises every morning around 11:30, for eleven days, and the largest trout are suddenly pushovers, racing three feet in the tail of a pool for even a sloppily dragging fat fly, I am seduced into the delusion that I have mastered this little game completely, that all chances from now on will be easy.

Every morning, after we descend from the last bench, we head

left, past the last sections of the East Branch, past the Paranoid Pool,
with its lithe and nervous shadows. My head is filled with memories
already. There are a dozen spots I want to fish. Memory mingles with
expectation and my new powers make anything possible. I have not
tried the fish in the Paranoid yet but I consider smugly that even these
are not safe from someone with my brilliance.

Ah, the Paranoid Pool.

There is still that.

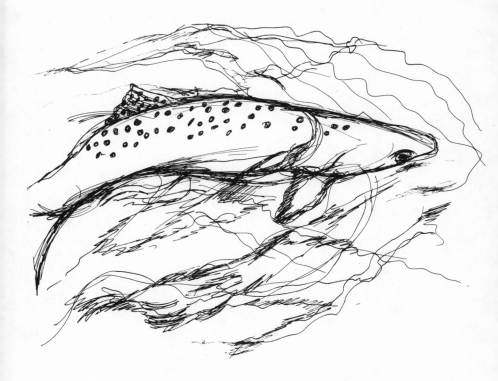

3

The Big Fly Comes

Nothing stirs a fly fisherman's heart like the presence, suddenly, of a big fly. Here is something that will raise the largest, wariest fish—just as I am raised, unfailingly, to a properly presented chunk of strawberry shortcake, or even one that is served gracelessly, with a rude abruptness. If there are huge trout in the river or the pond, you'll get them then—when the big fly comes. You feel it, electrically, even when there are no fish showing.

I was driving up the Gallatin Canyon many years ago and was suddenly faced with a front window splattered so richly, so yellowly, with bugs that I had to pull over, squirt soapy water up on the pane, and turn on the windshield wipers full blast.

"Holy cow!" I shouted to the empty car, never having seen bugs this big before. "It must be the salmon fly!"

A couple of inches long, full of yellow juice, with wings like a hummingbird's: it could be nothing other than the giant stonefly, *Pteronarcys californica.*

The Gallatin, though, was three feet high and chalky from a heavy rain the day before in the valley of the Taylor's Fork. Above, in the meadow section—which I raced to, skittering on the backs of thousands, tens of thousands of salmon flies—there were no flies whatsoever. Still, I had seen them—and they had sent me into shock. And so did those next ones I saw below Varney Bridge on the Madison River, fluttering in ones and twos above the water, several days after the "point of the hatch" had passed through, a few lunatic fly fishermen still rushing hither and yon, glassy-eyed, shouting "Where is it?" and "Has the point gone through?" It's often hard to

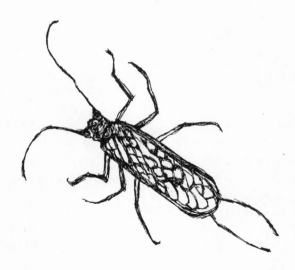

tell, when these flies or some other outsized insects are on, which goes crazier, fish or fishermen. Charlie Brooks once told me about a fellow who hooked himself through both lips with a Sofa Pillow during the first hour of a float, pinning his mouth shut. So hooked to the big-fly madness was he, so oblivious to all else, that he fished all day through a huge salmon-fly hatch with that large stonefly imitation reducing all speech to tight-lipped grunts. When his float pulled out at Ennis, his face was bloated beyond recognition and he had to be rushed to a hospital. A friend said, when I told him that story, that the guy was "a *real* fisherman"; but I think he was just a lunatic caught in the big-fly madness.

Before limits and fishing methods were changed and special regulations initiated, I several times saw boatloads of anglers fishing with spinning rods, plastic bubble floats, and live stoneflies pull out dozens of two-, three-, four-pound, and larger fish and then head upriver for another float.

Though there were no stoneflies on Spring Creek we once saw mysterious clusters of stonefly wings along the shore and could only assume that small birds had eaten the bodies and left the wings. I never saw a Spring Creek trout take a giant stonefly, though why they wouldn't I can't tell.

But if there was no fishing to the big stonefly hatch, we got something in its place. For a week and a half, always starting at just about 11:30 and lasting for no more than an hour and a half, we got a modest hatch of western Green Drakes, with some Brown Drakes occasionally mixed in. The fly was an honest #10 but better imitated by a #12, tied parachute-style and with an extended body. We also had very good fishing with a very green cut-wing fly with soft green hackle.

Herb and I had been driving downriver from the South End Pool, slowly, watching the water, the fifth or sixth day of my visit, when

I saw a splash rise that was too heavy and "wet" for a rise to the small Pale Morning Duns that we'd seen all morning, that were coming steadily now, all day long. The rise was even too splashy for a rise to a good-sized fluttering caddis. We were seeing more and more of these now, too—but this was different.

I pointed, Herb stopped the Suburban, and we both got out quickly and walked toward the water. For a few moments we saw nothing. Then we saw a Green Drake, perched high on the surface, float down the center of the pool like a stately sailboat, buffetted only slightly by the breeze. We pointed at the same time.

Herb said that he hadn't seen any drakes for four years; there had never been many of them. It just wasn't a reliable hatch on the river, like the Pale Morning Dun.

A few seconds later a trout rose noisily and we smiled and nodded and went quickly back to the car for our gear. I was in a state of high anxiety and barely managed enough composure to change the 6X for a long piece of 4X and to tie on a Para-Drake by the brilliant Jackson Hole tier Jay Buchner. Even then, I broke or slipped the knot twice.

A fat rainbow, one of the few in the river, took my first cast boldly and I took three more good fish within the next half hour. Herb did even better—five browns, all big dogs.

There is something quite magical about these big flies: not only do they raise the largest fish in the river but they'll bring them into a kind of bacchanalian frenzy at times, with otherwise sober fish losing all caution. On Spring Creek I saw a fish streak a full two feet in the slack tail of a pool, dorsal and body creating a wake that might be mistaken for that of a muskrat, to capture a drake that, in another moment, would have slipped into the next pool. The large fluttering fly makes pushovers, dumbbells of the wisest old trout, puts them into a frame of mind that can only get them into mischief. Everything, suddenly, is alive: sparrows and kingfishers, swallows and nighthawks dive-bomb and swoop, hesitating in flight, taking every drake they can capture. There are dogfights as the birds vie for the choice flies. And my hands shake and I snap off a couple of flies, and then some old alligator of a trout lunges a couple of feet and takes a natural right next to my imitation. I've gotten so riled, so lost in the sensual music, that several times when a truly large fish has taken the fly, lurched off upstream, and scooted under an overhung bank, I've quickly snapped it off, Shockgum leader or no. Then I'm too nervous to tie on a new fly properly, unsure whether to use an improved turle on the big fly or a double-loop knot I just learned or settle for the clinch, and, my eyes sewed to the water, looking for more flies, I'll fall into a muskrat hole, break my rod or my kneecaps or my tippet, tie on still another fly, and cast madly as I sink down further into the mud.

It's a crazy time.

I can't say I don't like it.

But I'm unhinged by it. It makes me a clown.

The British have what they call simply The Mayfly, with a capital M, a variety of our Green Drake but a bit larger; I've seen the great *Hexagenia limbata*, the largest of the mayflies, on lakes and I understand that in Michigan, where it's called the Michigan Caddis, the dusk fishing to this hatch can be extraordinary. The *Hexagenia*, a mayfly, is for some reason called a caddis, and the *Pteronarcys*, a stonefly, is called the salmon fly.

In the five years I fished the "Wilderness" section of the River Kennet in England, I never saw more than a mayfly or two, though I was once there on a ferociously windy day that marked the last day of the spinner fall. Each of those five years I'd arranged a business trip to coincide with that hatch. The closest I got were the reports from John Goddard, who told me many times about the big fish he'd taken

during The Mayfly, several times picking off four or five fish from a single pool, taking them one after the other, without disturbing the others, like playing Pick-up Sticks.

I saw the *Hexagenia* hatch only once, on a Connecticut lake. Larry Madison and I were in a canoe, cruising the flat water just at dusk, trying to make as little fuss on the glassy surface as possible because the ripples spread out quickly and kept going for fifty feet. We were sixty or seventy yards from the shore, against which rhododendrons sparked in bright pink. For an hour we had seen no flies; then, against the tree line, I saw some birds swoop, hesitate in flight—in the bug-taking mode—and zoom off. You always see the birds first: on rivers, in salt water, everywhere, they are the great harbingers of fish feeding.

Soon we saw, a hundred and twenty feet ahead, some of the large bugs hovering above the water or flat down on the glassy surface. Larry said that the fly had been on for four or five days already and that surely the fish knew exactly what to do with them. You could see a fly turning and writhing, twisting and struggling on the surface, trying to break free of its nymphal shuck, and then a slow slight wake from about six feet away would angle toward the fly, approach it deliberately, and then take it with great slowness and delicacy, almost as if the trout were pulling the great fly down by its legs.

Large flies these might be, but this was much tougher fishing than I had imagined.

The flies were sparse but now and then you'd see one flutter for a moment and then come to rest motionless on the surface, moving only slightly when a breeze came up. You could watch for four or five minutes, keep your eye locked on one particular fly on the surface, and it was amazing that nothing would come to such a dinner call. But then, usually just beyond Larry's considerable casting range, there would be a quiet rise. You had to use a pretty good imitation and a very light leader, since the fish had plenty of time to examine your fly, and you had to lay the fly delicately on the water at sixty-five feet or more, or the fish would spook. Without current, you had to cast toward where you thought a particular fish might go, though they could not be counted upon to go in straight lines.

For an hour we did not get even a good cast to a feeding or cruising fish and I could feel the tension building in me, as it always does when there are big fish to be caught and the fishing is difficult. These were obviously very large browns; Larry thought they might go twenty-four inches—and since they were lake fish, minnow-fed, they were deep-bellied. They were obviously taking these big flies— nothing else would have brought them up thirty-five feet to the surface in a clear deep lake like this, and in fact Larry said they mostly fed near the bottom and were unavailable to the fly rodder. I saw one fish clear the surface, coming up after a fly that, at the penultimate moment, took flight: the fish was long and dark and fat.

When the sun finally slipped below the tree line, Larry said he thought we might now take a fish or two. The air was cooler, the fish had lost a bit of their caution, and we had the cover of late dusk. I got five or six tense casts to feeding fish before 9:00 but was usually short of the rise, late, or too harsh with my cast. Larry suggested I try his rod, which was rigged with both a dun and a nymph. At first I said that I'd like to stay with only a dry; then, in frustration, I agreed to try it once or twice. On my first cast with it, in the general direction of a wake, I had a very sturdy take on the underwater fly. The fish was heavy—of the sort that you're afraid to test at first—and headed without delay for the bottom, in no particular hurry, scared of nothing. I got it on the reel, let it take line, and babied it, since I could not imagine it getting anywhere near obstructions in such deep water. Anyway, I've always found trout in lakes more difficult to fight than trout in rivers, despite the common philosophy on this subject; fish in lakes seem stronger, perhaps because they don't have to fight the current part of the time. Their range of operations is less limited. And they can travel in any direction freely—not against or aslant a current.

Larry said I was being too gentle with the fish, that the leader would hold, and I brought back the rod as much as I dared. But the fish simply kept going down and away from the boat, with that same heaviness. "Harder," he said, and continued with a brief lecture about how most fishermen didn't realize quite how much steady pull they can put on a line without the tippet breaking, and I leaned harder and suddenly the line was weightless.

The dropper leader had pulled loose.

Now, eight years later, I still get a twinge of anxiety when I think of that great fish I never saw, and I never fail to tell Larry the importance of careful knot-tieing, to which he responds that a *steady* pull is not the same as a jerk.

Grasshoppers—especially in those years when there is practically an infestation of them, or at least enough to get trout up high in the water, near the meadow banks, waiting for them—can provide this kind of big-fly excitement. Sandy Bing and I fished a meadow spring creek when the field it ran through was thick with large dusty hoppers. When the late-August afternoon wind came up they began popping into the water regularly, like hailstones in a flash storm. They'd float a foot or two and then these fat browns would come up slowly and take them with a smack of satisfaction, like a fat man popping his twentieth cherry bonbon, knowing its taste, full of Pooh-like expectation, happily addicted.

The high-riding Joe's Hopper would not take fish on this glassy water—not unless you trimmed its underside—but the Jay-Dave Hopper was lethal, with its low profile and legs spiked down to break the surface. Big flies need some characteristic shape or color or feature on which the fish will key; for grasshoppers, I think, the yellow underbelly and low profile and pencil-stub shape and surely the down-spiked legs are critical.

That afternoon I'd chuck my fly upstream as close to the near or opposite bank as I could manage, and those dog-sized browns would slip up after it and take it without hesitation. I won't brag about how many I took. By the end of the afternoon I merely sat on a high bank where I could get a good look at the show and watched still more hoppers flip and plop into the water and in a few moments disappear in a little spurt of white water.

And then the wind died down and the air chilled under a pewter sky and the river grew quiet.

On Spring Creek the drakes would stop every day after an hour or so and the river, everywhere, would look as if it did not contain a fish. But for that one explosive hour or hour and a half, every day for eleven days, we had astonishing fishing. With that first spurt rise we knew what was about to begin, and until the last two days—when the hatch simply petered out—it was great fun to see good fish come to the big fly, to these prodigies of nature that produced such hysteria in bird and trout and me.

The Nursery was spectacular, both with the Green Drake emerger and the dun: I couldn't believe how many fish it held—we caught fifty or sixty from that one glorious bend pool during the hatch. I'd learned the currents better by now and cast with a big upstream loop. The fish would take the fly with an abrupt and splashy rise, thrusting water out in every direction, and then they either bore heavily toward the bottom or headed downriver.

One morning, in one S curve after another, I must have taken more than a dozen good fish while the hatch was on—mostly in the foam line that traced the far bank. The trout could not resist the fly and several were as large as any I'd yet taken on a dry fly. They'd

streak across the tail of a pool for the fly, take it after it had started
to drag; they'd gulp it savagely in the riffles, sucking it down with
great satisfaction, not thirty feet away, in areas where you couldn't
come half as close to such fish when the big fly was not hatching.

As the hatch progressed I began to watch and wait longer, to
choose specific fish. I felt a greater calm building in me and a confidence that led me to look for fish in tougher places. I was not
especially interested in catching much larger fish—the ones I'd caught
were quite large enough—but in finding and fishing to more interesting fish.

Toward the end of the hatch, I found a very good fish rising in a
narrow channel—no more than a foot wide—near the upper end of
the West Branch. The river swept around one of the sharpest bends,
then hit a massive boulder flush in the center of the streambed and
split distinctly. One section swept broadly around the outside and
formed a large, rather deep pool. In the center of the streambed, below
the boulder, silt and rocks had built a bar to only three or four inches
below the surface. The far run, against the inside bank, was fast and
shallow and quite narrow. At first I thought it too small to hold a truly
good fish and concentrated on the pool.

But out of the corner of my eye I thought I saw the telltale spurt
of a rise to a Green Drake and looked hard at the narrow channel.

Nothing rose, but something in the conformation of the bank
held my eye: it was sharply undercut. The water rushing around that
inside corner had clearly worked back a full foot or more into the
root-growths and mud. Herb had told me that a friend in a scuba outfit
had once explored some of these undercut features in Spring Creek
and had reported that they were catacombs: a man could get lost for
a week in one of them. They went back for twenty feet in some cases.

I had had a good morning of fishing and felt very content with
myself so I sat down and stared hard at that strip of riffled water and

ten minutes later saw the definite splash of a heavy fish turning and taking a big fly in broken water.

I couldn't cast from my bank because the strong near current, then the big pool, and then the narrow fast strip would cause drag, so I headed downstream to find a crossing place. I had to walk a quarter of a mile before I could get comfortably to the other side, then walked slowly upstream without disturbing the water, staying just at the edge of the main current. When I got to the bottom of the bar, I crouched and started to duck-walk, to keep my profile low. About sixty feet away and fifteen feet out from the bank, I stopped, checked my fly, wondered whether by now the hatch was over, drew out enough line, duck-walked another ten feet closer, and cast onto the high grassy bank below where the fish had risen.

This was the last Green Drake I had with me and I did not want either to return to the car or ruin the run; on the 5X leader I knew I couldn't pull too hard, so I made a looping roll cast, a gust of wind caught it, and miraculously the fly came free.

I still hadn't seen the fish rise again.

The hatch might well be over.

I stepped a couple of feet to the left, into the edge of the deep pool, so I could get a better angle on my cast, stepped another few feet upstream, made a false cast up toward the boulder, shot out the line, and saw the tuft of feathers alight at the head of the run, an inch from the bank. The fly picked up the current at once and immediately dragged. I resisted stripping it off the surface and waited until it came down far below the fish. Then I simply stood still and watched the run carefully. In five minutes there was a spurt of water: the fish was still dining.

I cast again, put a snaky S into the line, saw the fly alight four feet above where the fish rose, saw it pick up the current, hug the far bank, and float freely over the right spot near the drooping grasses.

The fish took the fly in a rush and, happily for me, plowed into the heart of the run.

Then it went under the undercut bank and I urged it out, pulling back with steady pressure. Then it jumped: twice, three times in succession, high above the bank, smashing the water when it fell. It was too large a fish for that narrow run but it was determined not to leave it at first; had the fish simply gone up and around the corner I'd have lost it. And I'd have lost it if it had bolted directly downstream when the fight began. When it finally started to plow downstream, it was too late; I followed it easily along the bar until the bar began to lean into deeper water, and when the fish was swept around the next bend I had to stumble for a moment for firmer footing but, rod high and a little breathless, I managed to stay in touch.

In the next pool it slowed, wallowed, dashed off twice, each time with less force, turned a bit on its side, and I had it.

The fish was better than twenty-four inches—the largest trout I'd yet taken on a dry fly—and quite fat. Herb, who had been watching at least part of the time, estimated the fish weighed close to five pounds. "Well done," he said. "Well done."

Then the big fly stopped coming and for a few days thereafter the fish were not nearly so accommodating. There were PMDs every day but they often floated the length of a pool unmolested. The fish were subdued. They had lost all caution for more than a week; during their binge they had allowed themselves to be caught with clumsy casts, poor approaches, leaders the size of cables.

How I'd loved that electric moment when the big fly first appeared, and when we saw the first big fly every day, when I knew the kind of fishing we'd soon have.

And how I appreciated the time, after eleven days of such fishing, when I knew I would now have to earn each fish by so much more careful and skillful fishing, with a fly the size of a gnat.

4

Some Very Minor Spring Creek Tactics

The Green Drake nearly spoiled me rotten. During its hectic presence I became careless again about my casting, about my position, about whether or not the trout took me for a cow or thought they were making huge plump herons this year—and mostly it did not matter. If a trout had the sweet tooth for a drake, if it seemed so determined to risk its skin to get one, I could understand: I feel that way about duck-liver pâté, country style.

When the big flies stopped coming, we were already into July and the weather had grown bright and hot. Whatever new dramas were in store for me on Spring Creek, I knew they would be less generous. I knew the fishing would be harder—more exacting and more focused.

And every morning, as we headed to the right when we came down the last bench, I knew that soon I would have to contend with the likes of the Paranoid.

Every other element of fly fishing is dependent upon your finding a fish that is not scared, that you haven't been heavy-handed or -footed enough to send into shock. The right fly, the most delicate leader, the perfect cast all avail nothing if you've already put a fish into a state of acute fear and trembling.

From the beginning, it had seemed to me that this was one of the keys to Spring Creek; I knew it, painfully, the first time these trout flew from me, as from the plague, before I even got to cast for them. They saw me. Whatever the angles of refraction, the precise shape of the skylight on the roof of their world, their eyes knew me. The wraithlike forms were all aquiver. I felt exposed, gaped at, like a hooker, in crimson, in an Amsterdam window.

I accepted that I could not catch fish in the slick below the second large pond on the East Branch when they bolted before I got my fly line in the air; I suspected before too many defeats that only Herb could catch fish in the Two Islands Pool. I declined to engage with some of the trout I saw, thinking, "He's impossible. Period." And this attitude didn't change for several weeks.

Part of the problem, of course, is your distance to the fish, measured against how far you can see and how far you can cast. I have no interest in approaching to within speaking distance of a trout and I also cannot cast out an entire fly line and let it and the fly drop to the water like a feather. Some place between these distances, I want to be able to see the fish I'm after (before it sees me), reach it with my cast, and present the fly in a way that does not shock the poor speckled thing into an afternoon of locked jaws.

Stealth, which I had neglected during the Green Drake hatch, which I had begun to learn my first few weeks at Spring Creek, was the key. At well more than two hundred pounds and as short as a

1950s basketball guard, becoming invisible to trout was not the easiest problem for me to solve.

Herb had warned me not to wear very light or bright clothes and I didn't; some weeks later, a guest wore a freshly pressed white shirt, on the best day of fishing I've ever had, and caught nothing. Herb couldn't get that white shirt out of his mind for a week; he liked he who had worn it, but I kept hearing that image appear, with a great grumble and sigh, every time he spoke about stealth and "approach." I wore tan and I'm sure that wasn't the trouble.

Speed and carelessness were. I had always buffaloed along trout streams at a terrific clip and that's what I'd started to do here. By nature restless, I always walked quickly, waded hard, covered as much water in as short a time as possible. I've known some excellent fly fishers who fished this fast, though never as coarsely as I did at my worst, and caught more than their share of trout. Art Flick was one. He was quick as a marten or a mink. He preached that you couldn't catch a fish if your fly was not on the water, and that the more water you fished the more fish you'd catch. He fished pocket water, broken water, fast water, runs and riffles, places where the trout required much less delicacy from its pursuer. Yet even on such tumbling freestone rivers, Art rarely put down fish by first polluting the water with shadow, vibration, and sound.

Spring Creek was less forgiving. Some enemies of the trout came from within the water, like the otter, but most came from above, like the heron, the merganser, Herb, and me. The mischief came in at the eye and through the nervous system. Anything that moved above the surface, in the alien element of air, was a threat; the trout were used to that surface of the water, their roof, having a particular mien. When something moved in a way they were not used to—a figure breaking the glint of the sun, a fly line false cast once too often (which might be once)—they darted crazily around a pool and ceased all feeding for an hour.

The object here was to have your fly on the water less, and to fish less water, not more.

During that second week I found the Second Bend Pool on the East Branch, which we had not yet fished. The water here made a turn of more than ninety degrees and entered a long flat stretch. The first couple of times I approached it *in* the water, thinking to get below the line of the high banks. But I could get no closer than seventy or eighty feet before I saw huge wakes head upstream from the shallows into the deepest part of the hole. That first time, when I knew I'd troubled the pool, I kept going, so I could see what I'd spoiled. I was astounded to discover a huge head of fish, from ten-inchers on up and up and up, skittishly finning as far from me as they could get, hugging the bottom.

Then I tried creeping up on all fours, right to the bend, where I could look up it and cast with care; again I spooked them all, as soon as I sat up on that high bank. Even when I tried to wait them out from that position, my shadow fell across the pool and they stopped feeding before I could cast.

Finally, on Tuesday, I crossed the river far below, came up low on the inside of the turn, sat down on that inside rim below the bend, about forty-five feet downstream, and fussed for a half hour with my leaders and flies.

I was in no hurry and it was pleasant to sit there, tying on a fresh 6X tippet, trying a new head knot Herb had taught me that was intricate but stronger than the clinch or turle, glancing up to the vast sky now and then when clouds passed in front of the sun.

When I looked out to the bend again, the fish were feeding vigorously in the center current—four or five of them. There were plenty of Pale Morning Duns on the water—specks of gold glinting from the sun—and the fish were clearly on them. I cast sidearm, to keep the line low, held my seated position, and hooked one on the third cast. I got it out of the main current quickly, then downstream a few moments later. It was another of those nice eighteen-inch fish and it did not come in readily, but the fight was below me and five minutes later I had it close and extracted the fly with my hemostat. I took time to fuss with my fly, take a bit of weed from my leader, and then, when a fish came up I cast again. In ten minutes I had another good fish.

I took three fish from that pool and was hooked to the fourth, the largest, when it bolted upstream and around the bend. There was nothing to do but stand up and follow it, and I did this and eventually caught the fish. But the moment I stood, all rises stopped and did not come back.

A day like that did perfect wonders to my ego. The Green Drakes might have set me back, but I was on course again. And I began to think of all the little gestures that made such success possible: the dozen ways Herb had taught me to avoid drag; the steady loss of tolerance for my chronic sloppiness; the change from an easy reliance upon the Hairwing Coachman and the Humpy to flies that imitated an actual insect; the gradual elimination of lesser patterns for the few that worked much more of the time—a parachute PMD on a #17 hook tied by Al Troth, a Sparkle Dun, #18, tied by Craig Mathews, one of Dick Talleur's new cut-wing-style flies.

I gave up the Hairwing Royal Coachman, that lovely Christmas tree of a fly, reluctantly, the second week I was at Spring Creek. It had been the best of all-purpose flies, the equalizer, the great prospector. Some said it imitated an ant; even Preston Jennings said it made a good version of the *Isonychia* on the Esopus; but I think it imitated *some*thing only by chance. I had fished it because I could see it and because it took fish. Now I wanted to know why a fish took a fly.

Each of my new flies worked a little better in one place than another. And each day was linked to the previous days by memory— so that on each I felt better able to use what I had learned, was better able to bring just what I needed rather than a whole arsenal of paraphernalia, was more practical, more economical, more steely sure of myself.

I had learned to identify not only the hatch but the stage of the hatch on which the trout were feeding. When the PMDs came, the fish might still be on the nymphs, or they might want floating nymphs, with only an occasional dun. In the clear water I could watch their movements, see them tip up, watch that white mouth open or a snout come fully out of the water. On a windy day, they often preferred knocked-over duns; spinners might be on early or late, and might be mixed with newly hatching duns, though the trout preferred one or the other. Gradually I was traveling deeper into the mystery of it all, traveling with tools that better enabled me to experience what there was to be experienced.

On Wednesday of that week I had not been able to keep the trout from my fly. In the deep bend pools and on the flats the flotilla of Pale Morning Duns slipped downstream like miniature golden sailing ships, and the fish took them readily. I got three good fish that morning and I even got a large fish from the tough South End Pool, casting backhanded, fishing from behind a high tuft of grass on the right-hand point of the pool.

There were fewer and fewer pools now from which I had not taken a few good fish.

Thursday was another steady string of little triumphs with decent and difficult fish. I felt more and more confidence in all those delicious skills that combine to make a complete fly fisherman. Spring Creek had taught me. I had had to learn or I'd have gone fishless. My knots, some of them new, held. My reach cast and my plop cast did what reach casts and plop casts are supposed to do. If I didn't pick the right fly on the first pick, I picked it on the third or fifth or tenth pick, but I picked it. I had no tailing loops or ripped waders; I didn't fall in; the deer flies—increasingly annoying—took a few days off to visit the next valley.

I had still not caught another truly huge fish but I felt satisfied by a day without mishap, without a trout that I could not raise. I felt very superior, indeed—a quiet smugness that doesn't have to brag or boast or flaunt its clearly superior achievement. You spend thirty-odd years at something and you hunger for such mastery now and then, even when it puffs your brain, raises a lump of pride the size of an egg on your ego.

I felt so good about myself that I decided to diet and took along a couple of bright-green Granny Smith apples instead of elk sticks, like a good boy.

And then the next day began much like the others. We started in a run toward the end of the Junction Pool, below the Paranoid Pool, and I promptly nailed a bright brown of about eighteen inches on the third cast. It took a #18 Pale Morning Dun, tied with cut wings, brilliantly offered. I felt so confident that I sat down on a rock, got out my green apple, and was going to watch rather than rush. There was no hurry. I could see a dozen fish rising now above me, in the Paranoid Pool, and I'd watch them awhile. This might well be the appointed time for me to master this pool, too. In fact, with all the activity, perhaps I ought not to watch but ought to start in with them right away, while they were in such a happy mood.

So I put my apple, with its two bites taken, into an inside pocket of my vest and determined to contend with these fish at once. I worked myself into a good position near the far bank, to fish the far run from the right first. I began, as the books advise, with the lowest trout—and promptly lined it. Still, the fish soon started to rise again and my next cast, an upstream reach, worked well. The Pale Morning Dun slipped neatly toward the fish's feeding position, came closer, and went directly over it. "It's the cut wing," I thought, and promptly changed to a parachute style. Nothing. And nothing on three more casts. Curious. No matter. The fish kept rising and I'd get one in a few more casts.

But I didn't.

I changed flies twice more, then put the trout down and began to cast to another good fish, somewhat upstream. Nothing doing there either. Good fly, decent cast, good float—and nothing. Strange.

Most strangely, I couldn't seem to put the fish down for very long. In a few moments there were again a dozen rises, and I wondered which I should fish to. I remembered an old African maxim: "He who chases two chickens goes to bed hungry"—and promptly forgot it.

The fish across and slightly downstream looked especially keen

for PMDs, so I tried it, but after two tries I noticed that the one upstream four feet seemed to have slipped into a bacchanalian temper, so I started casting to it. Then to another. Then to the one near the point that Herb kept yelling to me to try. He had stayed in the car, the catbird seat for this little drama.

Six, seven different targets. Steady rises. I'd hit one, then the other, sometimes changing the direction of my cast in midcast, and then I'd change flies quickly and try another.

Sometimes I didn't change flies so quickly. My hands were growing just a bit shaky, and the deer flies had suddenly come back from the next valley, and one of them perched on my thumb while I tried to get the end of the tippet through the loops for the second time, for Herb's new head knot, and I squashed it with my other forefinger and lost the knot. That happened three times. The fish kept rising. These fish would have risen in the midst of a convention of herons. They had lost all caution.

Every new pattern I tried failed. I tried more—floating nymph, nymph-not-altogether-out-of-shuck, flopped dun, full spinner, half-spent spinner, #20 PMDs, #16 PMDs. Then another. And another.

I had to relieve myself but did not want to stop. Herb yelled, "The best one is near the point, just below the riffle." I tried it; I tried the happy riser downstream; I tried the one above the lip of the run, in the flat water. Nothing. Not a blessed look, let alone a take.

Finally I decided to fish on the near side of the island. Surely I'd ruined the two dozen fish on this far side for the next six months, though they kept rising.

Crossing the island on my belly, I got my vest hung—in four or five places—in the wild rose bushes and dragged my stomach and chest through the mud. I sometimes remind myself of a thrift shop when I'm *well* dressed; now I barely dared climb out of the rose thorns and mud for fear Herb would laugh himself silly.

Sort of stuck there, and thinking about the situation, and about fashion in general and particular, I remembered Isabelle's lovely comment in "A Wedding Gift": "I wouldn't let a fish see me looking like that." And then I remembered the day I went to an anniversary luncheon held at the Pierre Hotel for one of the great multinationals. I'd written a profile of the corporation and had been invited, but I had had classes that morning and had arrived so late that only one table was free. At it sat an especially unpleasant old woman—thin, long-headed, indifferent. She was the only other person at the table, though she was escorted by a very pretty young woman who stood at waiting behind her, fielding visitors who called the old crab "Dee-ahn, darling." I introduced myself. She did not look up. I spoke again, giving my name, telling her I'd written the book on this company. She would not acknowledge my presence. It was Diana Vreeland, long-time editor of *Vogue*, the arbiter of style, of which she deemed me to have none.

We sat for more than an hour together. I tried twice more. Nothing. She would not respond.

Nor would the trout.

Perhaps it was my sartorial lowness here, too.

Herb-the-Coach called out: "There's a very good fish near those two rocks, right in line with the car. Forget about the others." I saw it. It was a very good fish, indeed—and it was high in the water, dorsal out, stuffing its face with duns.

I decided to try the four near fish first and put them all down, one after the other. There were still plenty of Pale Morning Duns on the water and I saw four duns positively taken. Why wouldn't they have what I was pitching to them? I'd tried six or seven different duns, all the nymphs and emergers I had in my box, a small mottled caddis I'd seen, even a small Cream Variant. I had gotten not one rise in nearly two hours of hard fishing. I called to Herb and asked him to try them. He refused. I wished I hadn't acquired a bad bladder in my late middle age. I picked up a tailing loop on three casts that, each time, tangled my fly above the leader connection. I got loose line tangled hopelessly in the rose bushes.

While I untangled the cunning web of one such tangle, my line caught my hemostat and when I pulled my face was drawn into close proximity with my leader. As I disengaged line and leader and wild rose bush and hemostat, my fingers got pricked by the thorns in four or five places; I flinched, slipped, and put three thorns in the palm of my casting hand. A deer fly bit me good, just below my left ear. I couldn't untangle my leader, so finally I clipped off the fly and was about to tie on a new one when I realized that this was a sign. One looks for a sign at a time like this. For something. I wasn't as dumb as a slug. I needed a smaller leader point, that's what; I needed 7X.

With a long piece of 7X on I felt a sudden faint glimmer of hope in this Slough of Despondency. My first cast was true—just above the two rocks. My fly, one of the Sparkle Duns, came down over the big fish—perhaps twenty-four inches worth of wild brown trout. I watched the slate surface intently. The fish tipped up. The white of its mouth showed. It took the fly . . . and I snapped the fly off.

Now, in a fine frenzy, I cast everywhere at once, faster and sloppier, above, below, behind me in the run I'd fished first, and within minutes I put down every fish in both the near and far sides of the Paranoid Pool.

Throwing my hands up, I clomped downstream, straight through the middle of the near run; paranoid shadows swept before me; deer flies nipped me on the neck and wrist—they were everywhere; I exceeded the depth of my hip boots.

I paused for a contemplative moment when I was well below the run and turned to survey the damage I had wrought. As if by alarm, or by pure malice and contempt, more than a dozen trout had again begun to rise vigorously, no doubt perfectly sure that I posed no threat to their safety whatsoever, that I was not a heron, a merganser, an otter, a Herb, but simply a lunatic cow with a swishing tail.

At the car I paused to relieve myself. My green apple—twice bitten—slipped out of my vest and I went on it before I could swerve. Then I poured all the water out of my boots, opened my fly boxes and put them in the sun to dry, brushed off some of the mud, and climbed sheepishly into the car, leading with my chin. "I would have liked to see you catch those," I said to my pal, the masterful dry-fly fisherman, the coach.

He laughed deeply. "I enjoyed watching you *not* catch them."

It was Friday, as good a day as any to learn humility.

5

Wind and Rain

Periodically, blasting blue skies and sweet air, bursts of wind and rain drenched us under pewter skies. One moment you could barely find a cloud in the vast expanse of sky, and half an hour later the grasses would start to shake, the clouds would be everywhere above us, lead-tipped, and I'd be looking for a rain jacket.

More often than not we'd get sharp winds in midafternoon, real blowers that could last until early evening—or beyond. They did little to arrest the Green Drake fishing but the wind and rain blew the PMDs off the water and made casting with any accuracy impossible. Herb was not without resources when the wind came up. He dropped the angle of his arm to almost sidearm, added more authority to his back casts, and punched his line into the wind about as well as I could cast on a still day.

Rain, in most cases, merely made the fishing less comfortable. Herb didn't like to fish in it. But it had never troubled me when I was a teenager, when I'd fished with worms and spinners. I'd later fished a streamer well in the rain and once, on the Henryville water in Pennsylvania, someone had shown me that the odd Hornberg, on rising water, could be a killer.

I can remember a hundred days in the rain—watching the slow drip of raindrops from an old locust, and from an older oak that tipped slightly toward the river—watching wood beetles fall off and a white mouth come up from dark depths to take them.

Like dusk, wind and rain made the familiar unfamiliar, imputed mystery to what you thought you knew well, gave you concealment that the bright sun never stooped to do. Wind and rain also brought a rawness, a freshness.

Mari had begun to come to the river regularly with us. Pat had found her a canvas stool that held her supplies; she had a small portable easel on which to lean her pads; and she had been making a lot of watercolors that I liked. I enjoyed having her there, half hidden by the high grasses or up on the bench; I liked to turn from my fishing and see her working, discovering in what I found so lovely images that she was making hers. Other than the fear that she would get blasted by rain and even lightning before we could get the Suburban back to where she was working, I rather welcomed the differentness that the wind and rain brought.

Lightning—which streaked violently across the sky—troubled me most because I had heard of some poor bastard who, holding onto his graphite fly rod, got struck and scared silly. The few times I got caught away from the car I tossed my rod from me as if it had been a snake and simply lay face down on the ground.

For all but the lightest rains we simply took to the car. Herb would position it where we could watch the South End Pool or the Great Horseshoe Bend or one of the great flats, and we'd sit warmly inside, talking, watching, reading. Here Herb told me of some extraordinary fishing he'd once had on the North Shore of the St. Lawrence salmon river and how he'd have liked me to have a shot at it. It was a river where at least half the fish were caught on the dry fly. I wouldn't have minded that at all; my salmon fishing had been one week on an Icelandic river. It had intrigued me but it had not stuck— no more than tarpon fishing, where the guide found and stalked your fish, had stuck. I was being drawn more and more to the presentation of some reasonably accurate representation of a fly a particular fish was feeding on—to a specific feeding fish I could cast to, and had to gull. Nor was it mere custom or affectation to fish only to a fish that I could see, but practical wisdom; otherwise, I scared fish in such waters by casting where they were not, and then I was not ready when they suddenly went to lunch. When I accepted the restriction of not fishing blind, I began to learn more care and to see more. I began to think that what a trout saw when it looked up at the ceiling of its world was neither irrelevant nor trivial—certainly not on Spring Creek. In my childhood I had caught whatever fish were there by whatever means I could summon. Now I fished only with a dry fly, a limitation within a limitation, happily embraced.

One rainy day, as we sat near one of the bends on the West Branch, we saw the flattened shapes of Green Drake duns everywhere on the surface, and large trout, high in the water, wolfing every one they could get to. We got out for that and we caught just about every fish we pitched to, their yellow bellies distended from taking in so many flies. And once, late in the month, I fished a section of the West Branch curves during a heavy rain, punching a grasshopper into the wind, fishing the serpentine bends, the undercut banks, quickly, and pitching the fly down hard.

You could make do. Rain or wind did not mean an end to the fishing. And we could also talk or read or watch. You got a look at the river from a different angle; wind and rain changed the terms of the equation, as they do everywhere, and the new river was worth a hard look.

Almost always, whatever the weather, we went out in the mornings. But sometimes, if the afternoon wind was heavy or the rain too hard, we'd come back to the ranch early and spend more time indoors.

Herb had a tying table set up in the living room and on a rainy afternoon I might build a new leader here, using some of the fifty or sixty tools and glues he had there, along with plenty of spools of monofilament, a few spools of Shockgum, and plenty of braided butt material.

The shade for the standing lamp near the table was festooned with outrageous flies—an eight-inch-long squid, a mammoth sculpin, bass bugs the size of bats, woolly buggers and rabbit-skin leeches and Zonkers and even a plastic worm with hackle tied on at its midsection.

Herb read a lot in the afternoons when we stayed at the ranch and his reading was wonderfully eclectic: books about great adventure, strange and wonderful exploration in Tibet or along the North Shore of the St. Lawrence or in the West; all manner of books on fishing, from technical studies of stream plants to nineteenth-century treatises on fly tying; mysteries; spy thrillers; specialized works on the American Indian, on which he was a great expert.

And on a rainy afternoon we might have an early dinner. Usually we ate late—after the evening fishing, which got to be excellent, after the slow drive back, some cleaning up, a scotch or two, some talk. Pat was a superb cook. On the evenings we did not fish, we ate at eight or nine, and Mari remarked that the "continental dinners" were lovely but that it was fun, too, to eat before midnight.

* * *

One day in mid-July started brilliantly. At 9:00 the leaves of the cottonwoods were stone still; the sky was only slightly overcast, with predictions that the temperature would rise into the mid-seventies, that there would be no rain, that the wind would come from the southwest at only a few miles per hour. A perfect day. I could wade wet. I'd use only a visor, not a hat, and I'd wear my short-sleeved tan shirt.

Humming, I sat down on the front steps of the ranch house and took the rotted laces from my wading shoes, put in new leather ones, snugged them up carefully, and tucked my pants bottoms into the tops of my high socks. I added a dozen Pale Morning Duns from my stock boxes to the smaller ones I carry in my vest and prepared to sail forth. It was going to be a glorious day.

Twenty minutes later, before we'd finished loading the car, the wind started.

It blew the screen door off two of its hinges and toppled a cottonwood. Its steady, arrhythmic *whooosh* filled our ears. I knew Spring Creek would look more like an ocean bay than a spring creek. There was some serious talk about waiting until the wind died. Herb said he'd skip a morning and do chores. Mari advised that this was a terrific chance for me to stay at the ranch and talk to her—which she thought I might have forgotten how to do after several weeks of hard silent fishing.

She reminded me at some length about how compulsive I could be: fishing at Henry's Lake until the thumb, forefinger, and top of my casting hand were blistered crimson; how, on the scorching days here, when the sun hit the valley like an anvil and my face grew blotched with welts and my eyes and nose watered from hay fever, I just kept fishing. "I hadn't noticed," I said quietly. "I do other things in the world but when I fish I fish hard." I was about to mention that I admired those who are intense and driven, from Van Gogh to Theodore Gordon, who, without tricks, have genius—but I thought putting those two in the same sentence at this particular moment would be, tactically, a mistake.

In the end, I said I thought I'd just drive down to the river for a look; I'd probably be back in an hour. "That'll be the day," said Mari, frowning.

Wind is the bugbear of western fly fishing—and not so hot on eastern rivers, either; and it's positively lousy for any kind of saltwater fly fishing.

I've had my bad doses of it. Wind on Henry's Lake buffaloed a big orange woolly worm into the cartilage of my right ear; wind on a Utah bluegill lake stuck a thing with rubber legs firmly into my scalp; on Martha's Vineyard, using all my wit and strength, I managed to cast into the wind a full fifteen feet—and only later learned that no one did much better; they simply moved to the other side of the island. A friend, fishing from a float tube, was once blown across an arm of Hebgen Lake by heavy wind; he ended in a tangle of brush on the opposite shore and was contemplating the long walk back, around the arm, in flippers or bare feet, when he saw a helicopter descending in the nearby field. He began to call to them but then noticed that they were depositing something from a scrotumlike net beneath the plane. It was only a rogue grizzly—and my friend was persuaded to hide in the brush for an hour or so, until the wind died down, and then head back across the lake.

Spring Creek was a mess.

Small shorebirds, phalarope, swallows careened slantwise in the wind; weeds and detritus swirled in the pools; and everywhere the delicate spring creek looked angry, hassled.

I sat in the car alone, eyes peeled to the water. Perhaps I ought simply to head back up the bench for the ranch. The river did not, in truth, look very promising. It seemed a good time to chew on an elk salami stick, so I did, and then I munched another. One would have thought that the wind would tire of all its blowing. And perhaps it did. Within an hour and a half the sky cleared and the great western sun sparkled in a thousand places on the ruffled water; but then it started again and this time seemed to feed on itself: its steady, pressing, hissing rush continued, pushing against the grasses and the new willow shoots, whipping whitecaps onto the flattest pools.

Finally I left the car, rigged up my stiffest rod, and went down to the river. At first I cast directly upstream, into the muscle of the wind, but even the great power of the graphite rod I was using could not keep the line from its fluky, abrupt angles, the leader flopping madly, the fly dancing yards from where I wanted it to go, even when I punched the line low into the wind and felt so much more effective than I had been at this particular game five or six years earlier. Still, the fish weren't shy; I could get considerably closer to them—about twenty-five feet in places where sixty-five had been a minimum—and I managed to catch a few fish.

In a half hour the sky grew gray, the winds began to carry rain-spray, but the flies were hatching merrily now—PMDs and caddis—and the fish kept coming for them readily. Above me, swallows, with deft aerial gymnastics, caught their share of the hatching duns. Many of the duns on the water blew over, tilted on their sides, and I thought a hen-wing might work well for this. I had none but I jostled a cut-wing so it flopped to the side and took two fish on this theory.

Even a dumbbell like me is not dumb enough to keep punching a wind like that for too long without seeking a simpler route, so with great cunning I got upwind of the fish and cast down—or, rather, let the line sail with the wind while I guided the fly. I found a pool where a narrow chute of river opened into a large bend pool. The wind rocketed the duns across the surface, up against the far bank, and there they were caught in a foam line that, a few inches out, skirted the bank. This was an interesting situation and I kneeled and watched the drama closely. In an indentation in the bank, a trout had tucked itself below a clump of overhanging grass—where it had protection and a comfortable lie. The food lane brought it that continuous stream of duns for lunch and the fish picked them off steadily, so gently that it looked as if it was merely pressing its lips to the surface and sucking them down, intent on its feeding, oblivious to danger.

Had there been no wind I would have tried the fish from down-stream—though even on a calm day such a cast would have lined the trout or, if the fly was farther out, the fish would not have come for it. And the pool was too wide, perhaps one hundred feet across, and with too many tangled currents, to fish it from the opposite side.

In a strong wind—and perhaps under any circumstances—it was best to get slightly upstream so you could cast with the wind. If the drift was with just a bit of slack line, this might allow the fly to tuck into the feeding lane, then suck back as it came to the little eddy behind the tuft of grass. It was cold now; the wind was stronger and carried gusts of rain; my pants had pulled out of my high socks and my legs and chest shivered. I put six casts down and each time the fly pulled out, into the main current, just before reaching the clump of grass. The fish would not move for it. It had to be a good fish in a spot like that, I thought. Then I got out a cut-wing pattern, which I thought might get caught in the wind and flutter back into the little cove, perhaps with a bit of a nudge from me. I tried for five minutes to tie that fly on in the wind, with the cut wings wanting to fly off in every gust, my glasses sprayed with droplets of water, deer flies feasting on the backs of my hands. I'll bet they were surprised to find flesh out in this weather.

But then I got the fly on, made one light cast, guiding the fly into the wind, got lucky, and it dropped in the foam line, floated a couple of feet, tipped over from the wind (like some of the naturals), and scooted back behind the tuft where it was promptly taken by a brown that shocked me with its size—about eight inches.

It wasn't such a bad day after all, I thought, marching back upstream, shivering only slightly now. A river I'd fished hard for more than two weeks and thought I'd gotten to know reasonably well was suddenly not the same river; pools had changed and had to be fished in different ways; fish were in different places; you cast differently and had to strike differently. Long casts were out. Delicate casts were impossible. But interesting things were happening and I enjoyed seeing them. And I'd caught six or seven trout.

Walking to the car I passed the Two Islands Pool. There seemed to be a big commotion near where the water entered—a narrow passage where the water ran briskly and only half a dozen inches deep over some rocks before opening into the pool. Something—a number of somethings—was high in the water, gulping every dun or floating nymph that came down. Heads and dorsals, I guessed. I put my head to the water and could see a dozen of them.

I'd never taken a fish in this pool and had more or less consigned it to Herb, who always took a good fish or two here. But today, with the water ruffled from the wind, a slight rain and an overcast sky, with a good head of flies on the surface and a lot of fish feeding actively in broken water, I couldn't miss.

I still had on the cut-wing pattern and when I'd worked my way around the lower island and into position, I cast it up into the riffle. The wind still took my line in half a dozen different directions at once, but when it finally got to where it was going, the yellow cut-wing suddenly appeared on the surface and I watched it float down through the run wonderfully well, and then disappear. I struck and came up blank. Curious.

I could see tails and dorsals everywhere in the shallow run now and when I cast into their midst there was another good rise, I struck, and came up empty. Again I cast, and again watched the little golden dot alight and float a foot or two, then disappear. I struck quicker and quicker. Then I made a short hard strike, again came up with a loose line, roll cast the line out in a rushed, frustrated movement, could not see the fly, jerked it back hard to bring the line off the water for another cast, and felt a sharp tug.

All fly fishermen feel a special satisfaction when they take a fish where they thought they could not take one. It is the satisfaction anyone feels when he has solved a difficult logistical equation. Selecting the proper fly pattern and design, overcoming a stiff upstream wind, beating the drag built into twisted currents, solving a problem of approach bring a flush of pride—and the proof is always in the catching. A slight, smug, self-satisfied smile comes to one's lips. Anything—even losing weight—is possible.

I smiled a slight, smug, self-satisfied smile. I had never taken a fish in the Two Islands Pool and now I had one. I may not have hooked it, properly, on the surface, but I had one and it felt very good.

Only it acted a bit oddly.

It did not go out in a heavy rush of power; it did not sulk; it did not come crashing out in a leap of exaltation and bravado. It sort of zigzagged.

This, I soon learned, was because it was not a trout.

Thirty feet out, right at the surface, I saw the writhing form of a snake, close to a thirty-incher, *sssssssing* its way toward the opposite bank. The little golden speck that was a #18 cut-wing PMD was attached to its middle, as if the fly had been dragged, quite wet, and foul-hooked the reptile.

I do not especially like snakes and promptly lowered my rod so it could break off. But try as it might (and *I* might) the snake could not break the 6X tippet. Herb's ingenious Shockgum leader was having its most brilliant hour.

There was nothing to do but bring it in, and with constant

pressure I drew it closer and closer. But then what to do? I was in the Rockies and I had no idea whether the snake was poisonous or not, and, even if not, the closer it got the more I felt "zero at the bone." Not only would Herb's leader hold an especially large catch, but I could not un-catch it.

Closer and closer I played the snake. I gave it hard short tugs to bust the tippet, but the tippet would not break. I pointed the rod tip at the wretched thing and jerked, but the snake only turned and came swiftly toward me, so I stopped jerking. Out it zigged and in I zagged it, until soon the leader was to the tip of my rod and the snake much too close for comfort. I was sorely tempted to cut the leader where it joined the line but I had no replacement with me and Herb had taken more than an hour to build this one.

In desperation, I hoisted the reptile—wriggling and twisting—at rod's length and began a certain swinging, swaying motion that I thought might break it off at the tippet, launching it into space, but the 6X tippet held and the snake kept dancing at the end of the yo-yo-like contraption, swinging closer to me on each backswing after each time I swung it out. I was furious at Herb for being such a genius at leader construction.

In the end, I swung it high and far, so that the snake slapped down close to my feet, wriggled onto my pants, made me dance a little jig until I stepped back into some weed shrubs; I fell to a sitting position, saw the snake wriggle up my leg, levitated, and booted the leader harshly. Even then it did not break. But the braided butt must have rubbed against the rocks, for suddenly, as I tugged and high-stepped, it burst, and I kicked the snake into the water and galloped downstream, making a terrible commotion.

The wind and the rain were quite fierce now but I noticed, in the pond above the Two Islands Pool, that half a dozen absolutely huge fish

were prowling the windward shore, waiting for grasshoppers to be
blown in; I saw them take three. This was a clear, shallow pool, a
couple of hundred feet across, and the fish in it had been impossibly
difficult. Herb had pointed to some of the great wakes in the pondlike
area and said that, under the right circumstances, they were catchable.
I put a #8 Jay-Dave Hopper out where the big fish were cruising,
raised one of them, got a few hard looks, and then snapped off one
the size of a muskrat.

Then I worked my way a mile upstream, into the headwaters of
the East Branch, hoping to find a few sheltered places. I hadn't been
up here before and vowed to come back on a less blustery day; the
water was smaller, swampier, deeper, surrounded by muskrat holes
and soft banks.

The fishing was spotty—mostly short casts, not to feeding
fish—but I got a few small browns and felt very pleased with myself.
Then, in a small run, I saw a spurt rise and then another, and a few
good-sized caddis dancing near the opposite bank. I sat down, so I
could be very low and near the water and perhaps beneath the wind,
tied on a #12 Elk Hair Caddis, and cast it to the head of the run. The
fly came down pertly on the little chop and there was a good splashy
rise and I came up without the fish. But the fish took my next cast and
it proved to be the best fish of the day, a fat brown not much shy of
twenty inches.

By midafternoon, after six hours of it, I got back to the ranch. The
sun had come up and the wind was mild. Mari frowned and asked if
it had been worth the trouble, and said that she had worried about me
and had I been thinking of her, and though the gentlemanly thing
would have been to say I'd much rather have stayed back and talked
to her, I had to admit that the morning had had its surprises.

"Do anything?" asked Herb.

"Some," I said.

74   "Enough to go out in all that?"

"Maybe," I said. "Are there any poisonous snakes down there?"

"Not one," he said.

"Ever see snakes rising to PMDs?" I asked.

"Have some scotch," he said. "You need it."

30 June 1992
Craig & Nick

6

Big Fish

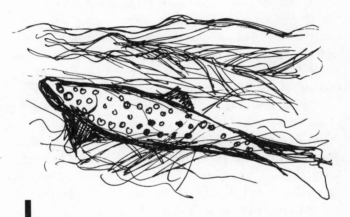

I had caught several large fish during the Green Drake hatch but I raised my two largest in the big pond above the Two Islands Pool on Pale Morning Duns. In both cases I'd lost the fish through stupidity. One took off in a tremendous rush of power and I simply broke it off, Shockgum or no. The other mistake was the product of letting my attention wander during some slow fishing at the pond. I had been casting and watching the tiny speck of gold on the slate water for an hour and I had not quite believed that I could raise one of the truly large fish whose wakes we now saw streaking through the pool regularly. I turned my head for an instant, the fish rose, I turned back at the slight sound, and in haste struck late and snapped it off. I think such fish are lost because the fish has already got going in the opposite direction and you snap the line rather than pull with a steady firmness.

I had seen a lot of large fish making wakes in the neck between two of the lower pools and spent one afternoon working my way into positions on both sides of it, spoiling the pool three times, and then, finally, fixing myself on one bank, sitting down for a half hour until the fish got going good, and then fishing slightly downstream to it, on a slack line. The fish came to the Pale Morning Dun readily and took me well into the backing—but it came back under steady pressure and at last I had it. I guess it was twenty-two inches or perhaps a bit larger, and I felt very proud of myself.

Big fish, really big fish, larger fish than you've ever seen before—except on someone else's wall or in a garish photograph—provide electric excitement, a sudden quick challenge to all you have learned in your marrowbones, and a relief from all smaller fare. And just as surely, they are a lure that hooks you to fish more. For something bigger. For a record perhaps. For a fish that has some claim to immortality. Which can be a serious business.

I know people—young and old—who live for such outsized fish. One cock of the walk is interested *only* in the biggest salmon. He is a big-fish fisherman of the first water. He's also a big fish in the art pool in which he swims and he only wants to catch big fish there, too. His talk is a litany of accomplishments; he always wants the newest, biggest, best, most; he does not "pick up a pen" for less than several hundred thousand dollars. And he generally gets the newest, biggest, best, most, which he needs, which back his advertisements for himself. He wants records and mounts; he is bored with less.

I would be too often dissatisfied if that's all I came to fly fish for—the big fish. Dreams would too often outrun reality. But there is more to those big fish, something not pathological. They nibble at my brain—albeit they're usually the fish that have gotten away. They stretch us, expand the circle that contains our sense of ourselves, the limits of some imaginative construction of what we can and cannot do. Roger Bannister spent years trying to break the barrier of the four-minute mile and then dozens did it; many fishermen catch permit regularly on the fly, though this was once rare; and more fly fishers hold larger trout than they dreamed could be held on a #20 dry fly. Big fish jolt us. They are bigger than life, or make life bigger. They swim in our brains for decades, long after lesser fare have faded— bigger, older, rarer, more difficult, unusual, commanding our hardest-won respect.

One chilly gray morning during the middle of the third week I'd been at Spring Creek, we came down the bench, headed right toward the Paranoid and Farrago pools, then drove up the East Branch to the big pond, which had shown more and more life lately.

It was a gray, trouty, drizzly, sullen day, and as I strung up my rod and put on my hip boots, I kept scanning the river, searching for a rise. The water was oddly alive. It had a mysterious energy to it. There was a slight mist on the water, turning gently, and the water was nervous here and there, with wakes and bumps on the surface that I knew were fish looking for food.

I took up a position I'd taken twice before, toward the uppermost section of the cove—sitting on a tuft of grasses just at the point, where I was able to cast upstream and allow the fly to slip down toward me and then past me at a snail's pace.

I sat quietly on my wet perch, rump wet and cold, and lay my rod across my knees, shotgun-style. There were a few golden spots on the surface, floating ever so slowly. My eyes began to flick everywhere across the surface, looking for a rise, a steady wake, a sign. I picked out individual mayflies and watched them float forty, fifty, a hundred feet. A half hour passed. The sky remained a solid mass of gray. Every fly I saw floated downriver unmolested.

Herb was fifty yards below me, in the middle of the pool, and though his fish would be farther out, he could cast twenty-five feet or more farther than I could.

We kept watching the water, not turning to the other, saying no more than a word or two to each other, a phrase, merely pointing. We both felt, in the gray silence, that something was about to burst. There was something about the way the fish were lolling, close to the surface, and the leisurely heavy nervous movement of their wakes.

And then, suddenly, a couple of trout started to feed.

There were three widening circles, widely separated.

We both pointed and grunted.

And then there were eight or ten or more fish up, high in the water, their dorsals out, taking the fly with an unhurried confidence. The slow rises, the slowly spreading circles on the flat surface, the slow, deliberate pinching and erupting of the water were heart-stopping. We were on one of the toughest pools on the river—a hundred and fifty feet across, perhaps three hundred feet long—and it was beginning to explode.

Here and there a dorsal fin or a tail slipped up out of the water, sharklike, and then there was a heavy wake—one hundred feet out— as a good fish moved close to the surface, less wary than ever now. And then there was another spreading circle.

My quiet patience began to give way to inner mania, which I struggled to suppress. The fish were still beyond my casting range and there was nothing to do but wait until they worked their way closer.

I heard line peel off Herb's reel as he drew out enough for a cast and then I paused from my own concerns to watch him cast toward a spreading circle.

I had a dozen versions of the PMD in my box but chose a #18 Mathews Sparkle Dun. In this especially flat, diamond-clear water the fish could examine the fly with critical care; I wanted the trout to see the body color, the silhouette, the Zelon tail or shuck.

The trick then was to cast an honest sixty or seventy feet from that sitting position—not panic and drop the back cast so it hooked the grass behind me—and to have the fly alight lightly a few feet above the feeding position of the trout, where it could pick up the minimal current and float without drag to the precise spot where the fish had taken its stand.

Miraculously, I made the impossible cast the first time. The fly fell perfectly and started its ever-so-slow float toward the spot where one of the trout was rising. I waited. The moment was charged with intensity. Someone might have kicked me in the kidneys, I'd have felt nothing. I leaned forward, waiting for the gold dot on the slate surface to disappear in the ring of that trout's rise. I muttered to the fly that it should not drag. It heard me. I waited some more. In this flat water, you could recite a couple of pages of *Paradise Lost* while a trout made up its mind, while the fly inched toward it. "He'll come to lunch," I thought. And then the fly floated merrily over the trout and on down the river.

Why? Why didn't the fish rise? There had to be a reason. Was the 6X leader too heavy? Was there imperceptible drag? Were the fish really taking the emerging mayfly and not the adult?

Herb got a good fish about noon, and then, a half hour later, I hooked something quite large and lost it, and then the water was quiet for an hour and we sat and fussed with our tackle. We'd taken no lunch along and were expected back at the ranch, but neither of us thought of eating. About two o'clock I had a delicate rise—no more than a pinching down of the water under my fly—and came up tight with a tremendous fish that race-horsed directly across the river so hard that I thought it would beach itself and go halfway up the bench. But the fish turned, jumped three times, went upstream, then down, well into my backing, and finally I urged it in. It was the largest trout I'd ever taken on a dry fly—a full twenty-five inches and perhaps six pounds, with a sharply hooked jaw.

Then, a half hour later, I took another, also a male, almost identical but a bit over twenty-five inches and a bit heavier.

That was quite enough—thank you—for a day, for the year, perhaps longer. I walked back to the big Suburban to fetch out a cup of lemonade, as an excuse for getting off the front line, as a way to try to stop the radical tremor that I had contracted in my right hand after that second huge fish. I didn't mind the tremor. It was a happy little nervous twitch, that's all, and it would stop in its own good time. One of my legs was trembling, too. I don't remember which.

I really didn't think I wanted to fish again that day. There was nothing better out there for me and I'd taken as much as my memory could hold. I'm always astounded when I read of someone catching forty, fifty, sixty trout in an afternoon, ten of them over such-and-such size. Why? Why continue? A few good fish make a day. More make an orgy. A flurry of fish-catching satisfies me completely. I don't want to catch every fish in the river. I don't want to "beat" my companion. I don't want to break records. That's the tournament mentality, and it makes the worst of the best.

But I could not help but watch.

Mari and Pat came down with a wicker basket of sandwiches. Herb laid down his rod and came up to the cars. And we both chose out what we wanted and began to eat. But even as we ate, our eyes could not stay away from the water. The PMDs were still coming; there were still snouts and tails and wakes everywhere. Something else was going to happen.

Mari tried twice to talk to me but I didn't look at her. I could not

haul my eyes from the water. Herb told her about the two big fish I'd taken. Pat got excited by this but Mari merely said, in a flat tone, "That's nice, for you, dear." And then, in a whisper: "You don't talk. We don't even have a platonic relationship."

I tried to explain to her what was happening on the pond, how it happened only infrequently, how this was a Day of Days. I kept watching the water. I was mesmerized by the water. I don't even remember when Pat and Mari left, or what I said, only that Herb was soon back on his perch and I was leaning on my arms in back of the Suburban, watching him intently.

He cast sporadically, when he saw a rise or a wake heading in a particular direction. He cast a low, fast, long line, and I thought how much like wing shooting this was, watching the direction of the fish, casting quickly beyond it, into its path, then waiting with great expectation. That wait, that hesitation, was devastating.

From where I stood I did not always see the fly alight on the slate surface of the water, and now and then I'd pour myself another lemonade or fuss with my reel or line. I felt very contented. I had caught a couple of remarkable fish and that, thank you, had been quite enough. But I was facing the river and whenever I looked up I saw it and Herb and watched until whatever little drama was being played was done. I was looking up when I saw a fish rise twice, then—with a wake—drift off to the right. Then it came back and took four or five PMDs. Herb watched, tense now, waiting to cast. I wondered why he was waiting so long. Did he want the fish to get good and confident? It was clearly a very big fish, but there were a lot of big fish in this pool and it was quite impossible to tell from the delicate rise and the wake quite how large this one might be.

For a few moments the feeding stopped. Then I saw the slight bulge and dimple of the fish, about seventy-five feet out, to the right, and then I saw Herb's rapid cast.

I saw his bright yellow parachute alight four or five feet up from where the water had pinched a moment before. The cast, with only one false cast far to the left, had been exactly on target. The rumpled leader started to straighten, the fly moved ever so slowly on a current you could not see, and I felt my heart leaning out onto the water, straining after the fly—my breath slightly irregular—wanting to coax the fish into taking.

That moment was more than six years ago and memory, for me, about fishing, always mingles with fantasy and dream. But this memory is too sharply etched not to have been real.

I remember the long length of line going back and then forward, and then shooting to a distance of perhaps seventy feet. I remember the #17 Pale Morning Dun parachute alighting with a final little somersault of the leader and then picking up what there was of current and floating slowly downstream. I remember the expectation and the wait. And I remember with perfect clarity—when I run the entire scene out in my mind, in sequence—the slight pinch and bulge of the flat surface . . . and then the sudden, immense, electric rush of force.

The trout took Herb's fly lightly and did not move off unperturbed by the prick, like the books say. The fish zoomed off like a bonefish—hard and fast and far, in a straight line, like any wild thing held; and then, two hundred feet up the long pool, it leaped once, erupting, exploding, splattering the air with bubbles and silver splashes of water.

"Bigger than I thought," Herb said.

He stood up now, intent, looking upstream.

"Parachute?" I asked.

Herb nodded.

I worried about the size of his leader point and asked: "Six-X?"

He nodded again.

After the jump the fish settled down to doing what a truly big fish is supposed to do. It moved off heavily, steadily, heading for the uppermost part of the pool, where the river pinched through the last narrow sections of land and broadened and slowed.

The fish was clearly larger—by a great measure—than the two fish I'd taken. Quite how large it was I could not tell. The fish was now well into the backing, perhaps three hundred feet upstream, and all you could see was the long expanse of buckskin fly line and then the smaller white backing, and at the far end a steady surge of water, as if a foul-hooked muskrat or a beaver or an otter was burrowing just beneath the surface. There was simply no way that this fish would not break off.

Herb's leader was decisive. He could not have held the fish without it. For with all that line out, and the fish making sudden moves to the left or right, the 6X leader would surely otherwise have broken. But it did not. The fish veered off toward the far bank and the tippet held. The fish slashed at the surface and I thought that surely now it was gone; but the line was still taut when the commotion stopped. The great trout came up twice more—hugely, splattering water high, shaking, then crashing back down—with ninety feet of fly line and 280 feet of backing between it and the fly rod, and the fish was still on, and heading still farther upstream, around the bend.

You could not begin to pressure such a fish on such tackle yet, but you could stay with it, subtly—lean into it, drop your rod tip when it jumped, lower the rod (as Vince Marinaro advised) when the fish ran, so the line came directly off a finely tuned reel, with less friction. With abrupt, deft, athletic movements, Herb managed it all.

But then I saw him fumble with his reel and lean forward awkwardly, his rod extended as far as he could extend it in front of him. Something had happened. Was the line tangled? Surely he'd lose the fish now.

The bottom of the pool here was muddy and pocked with muskrat holes. It would be treacherous to wade toward the fish, and to get out of the pool and walk up the brushy, irregular bank could be fatal to the fight in a dozen ways. No, he had to stay in the water, where he was, in that one spot, and he had to manage the fish from that fixed position where he stood. There were no other options, no other ways to save what was becoming a desperate situation.

I did not have to stay so far from the action so I had walked to a high bank upstream where I'd have a better chance to see the great trout. I trotted back now to see if I could help Herb with whatever problem he had. The problem was this: the fish had taken the last foot of backing and for a moment—fumbling with the reel, leaning forward—Herb was trying to reach out and secure another foot or two of line before the gigantic fish broke off, which surely it would do. The fish was at the very end of the backing and sort of wallowing there, not pressing forward, finally tired perhaps, after the run, the shaking, the acrobatics. The fish could not be pressured but perhaps it could be *urged,* and Herb leaned his rod back a bit, then dropped it and reeled, to regain another foot or so of line. But the line would not come back onto the spool; tied loosely, with a slip knot—the only carelessness in Herb's rig, or perhaps not—the line was circling the spool without coming back onto it. With the fish moving slightly toward him now, the line threatened to go slack.

Herb's fingers, fussing with the circling line, grew frantic for a moment.

Still leaning forward, he had to tighten the knot with his free fingers and coax line back onto the reel.

Well, that's it, I thought. A fly line and one hundred yards of backing hadn't been enough to hold this fish. If the great fish made a sudden move now, Herb would lose it for sure.

But despite the slack and the fumbling, the fish was still on.

Foot by foot Herb urged the gigantic thing back toward him,

regaining half, then three-quarters of the backing as the fish turned and headed heavily, at an angle, downstream. There was no urgency in its movements now; the fish was subdued, worn, if not yet quite beaten. It could be led without being forced. The process—now done by inches—required immense patience.

Back on the high bank I kept my eyes flicking from fisherman to fish. In ten minutes the trout was back onto the reel and I knew that it would only take a few more minutes before Herb had it at his side and would be reaching down to release it. I'd seen him handle the endgame flawlessly dozens of times.

The fish was near the surface now, canted to one side slightly, not twenty feet from me, and I could look down and see it with absolute clarity. I can see it still, all these years later. The trout was a full foot longer than the two I'd caught, thicker by far, more than double their weight. And it was nearly beaten. I have seen larger trout come from lakes, on leaders the size of cables; steelhead are larger, even stronger; and this was fully the size of a dozen Atlantic salmon I'd seen. Why did this fish seem then—and why does it still seem—the most prodigious trout I'd ever seen? Surely the light tackle—not an affectation but a necessity for luring such a fish—and the relative size of the fish to this type of fishing played their roles. But a two-pound bluegill, even a giant of its species, is still only two pounds of bluegill, a piker. This fish was a monster.

"It's heading toward the weeds," Herb said flatly. "Can't put more pressure on."

The big head came half up out of the water and shook once, and the leader held, and Herb coaxed it slightly, firmly, away from the weeds. I felt quite sure he'd keep the great trout out of the weedbed. I felt sure he'd take it now, with only thirty or forty feet of line out.

And then the fish went a couple of feet off to the right, into the region of the weeds, and was off—and I felt then, and feel now, years

later, as you must feel reading this, as all of us feel at such moments—
as if I'd lost a part of myself and would forever be searching for it.

Herb reeled in quickly, checked the end of his leader, and found
that the #17 golden fly had neither broken off nor bent straight, but
simply pulled free. "Didn't break him off," he said. He smiled, shook
his head, and said mildly, *"That* was a very big fish, Nick."

Now, so long afterward, I can forgive him his insouciance: a man
who could fight a fish so well and lose it with so little trauma had to
have caught a dozen that size.

I'd have punched myself silly.

7

Visitors

Mostly we fished alone and that was company enough for me, for I have never liked crowds, though I have always lived in the midst of them, and Herb and I had found a pleasant rhythm together that I did not like to break. Mari usually came with us now, and we dropped her off at a motif she wanted to paint and went about our business. Once she was perched on the top of the bench and I watched her all morning as I worked my way slowly around the first three bends of the East Branch. And often I'd see only her head, looking up then down at a watercolor or sketch, as she sat on a camp stool and worked. The landscape was working on her, too, and she was becoming more and more interested in the odd business that brought us here, fly fishing for trout.

When the skies were dark gray or bruited by dark-bellied clouds, I worried that she would get blitzed by rain or hail, or battered by the wind; and when the sun was high and hot, I worried that she'd get burned bright red or chewed by the deer flies. But as the days went on she prepared herself better and better, with bug dope and sunscreen and rain jacket, positioned herself where she'd be able to work for a good length of time, and she became part of the rhythm of a day, too—which I liked.

We'd rattle along the benches, pause at the last one, Mari might gasp and say something about the space, and then we'd head down to the river, thinking mostly about the fishing. There were still antelope in the fields but fewer now; the fawns were quick as the wind and very lovely. We'd seen coyotes in the fields and they surely would have gotten a few of the fawns.

The river, spring fed, had not dropped an inch, but it was beginning to take on some weed, and the carcass of the calf hit by lightning was more shrunken. Now and again when we passed the Paranoid Pool, Herb would pause and lean out and rag me with, "The apple tree will be sprouting soon," or "I wish it had been a sandwich."

After a couple of weeks Herb invited a few friends, and occasionally he'd accept a social obligation to let someone fish Spring Creek, though he resisted this firmly. The visitors made me think of restriction and of the relationship of use to biological health. Herb never had more than four rods on the river at once, and rarely that many; and he rested sections for days after they had been fished hard. Even four fishermen, he once told me, if they were skillful and fished long and hard, could put immense pressure on the fishery. Stewardship demands restriction, limitation; protected, a resource could maintain what it is and what it ought to be indefinitely, and not suffer that niggling, inchmeal deterioration that is everywhere a disaster.

Some of the people who came to fish with us were famous fly
fishermen or old friends of Herb's. Most were very experienced fly
fishermen, but others—however amiable—were simply not adept
enough for it. One extremely pleasant fellow forgot his glasses,
brought the wrong boots, and, in Herb's words, "couldn't cast to his
shoelaces." Herb worked patiently with him for more than an hour,
holding his arm to give force to his cast, positioning him at the
choicest corner of the Farrago Pool, where there were always fish
rising. No success. We had started late because of the visitor and
the morning seemed interminable. I went off for a half hour and
came back; Mari sketched, near me and then near the car—unable to
find quite the right place to work. Three hours, four hours passed.
We finished the one jug of lemonade. More time passed. Then Herb
drove us all upriver to The Nursery, where no one, ever, failed to
raise a fish or so. Nor did this nice fellow fail. With Herb's help he
raised four—and either struck early or late or too hard with them
all.

It grew to be 3:30, then 4:00.

"This is the worst day of my life," Herb said as we sat in the car
watching the fellow flail away. "The fish come up and he can't hook
them, or he snaps them off. It's like coitus interruptus."

I said I'd try to help him get at least a fish or two and started out
of the car.

"Miserable day. Miserable day," Herb muttered. "And I'm
thirsty."

"But you're being so nice to let him fish the river," Mari said
cheerily. "Think of the human values."

"You think of them," Herb said. "Say, Mari," he added, "you
wouldn't mind going down there and telling him you're sick or have
to go to the bathroom or . . ."

"No," she said. "I won't do it."

When I got to the man's side, I realized that it was practically

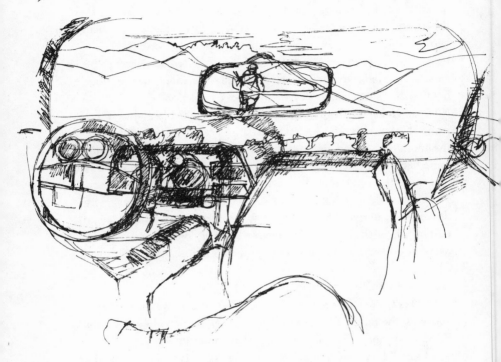

hopeless already. He had been beating the water to a froth and even these unwariest of Spring Creek trout would be under a rock, terrified.

"I'd love to catch just one of these beauties," the fellow said. "I'd stay here until midnight to do so."

I said I hoped it would not take that long, and thought of lunch. A man my size almost always thinks of lunch, especially at 4:16 in the afternoon. "Let's just wait a few moments," I said. "Change your fly and leader" (which would give the pool a chance to settle down) "and give it at least one more careful shot. This can be a very tough river, you know."

"I got six when I floated the Yellowstone," he said. "No trouble at all. This river *is* hard."

I clipped off the leader at six feet and shoved the whole lower section into my vest pocket; it was hopelessly wind-knotted and had two sweet little loops protruding, too. Then I constructed a new one, quite carefully, and then slowly tied on a #16 Humpy with a yellow belly. When the rig was ready he took it from me and back cast into the grass. I unhooked his fly and he whisked it by my ear and slam-dunked it on the water. Then he whipped it back and forth, whirled it around a few times, picked up a few new wind knots, and cast the fly down just beyond his shoelaces. I'd been in almost such a position before, many times, and it had bothered me a whole lot. But he was better than me. It bothered him not at all; he was having a fine time. I asked if he'd mind if I helped with a cast or two, he agreed, and we got out a couple of decent thirty-foot casts together. Nothing. The fish had gone down and I barely had the heart to tell him that they intended to stay down, perhaps for a week, and twenty minutes later I merely put up my hands and said, "They must have stopped biting. We ought to head back for lunch, I guess." It was 4:52.

"I guess I'll just try a few more casts," he said. "Had a late breakfast."

"We really shouldn't keep Pat waiting."

"A few more casts won't hurt," he said, with great glee. "This is wonderful. I just wish," he said with a happy childlike enthusiasm and wistfulness, "that I'd catch something, too."

At the car, Herb was leaning far back, in the passed-out-from-exhaustion-and-starvation-and-thirst position; his tongue was hanging half out of his head. It was 5:07.

"Herb thinks that perhaps, that maybe we ought to . . . well, have some lunch," Mari said, unable to stop laughing at the prostrate figure in the front seat.

"Your friend," I said, "will be just a few more minutes. He wants to make a few more casts."

Herb groaned. It was perhaps the longest, saddest groan I've ever heard.

Fishing catches an odd bag of us in its nets. A relative of Mari's from another part of the country visited us recently, and when I told him I liked to fish he shook my hand and said he was a brother fisherman. Then, confidentially, he told me about a surefire lure that I could use but was not to make public. It was a hollow plastic worm—with Alka Seltzer in its cavity, scented with anis. "Chartreuse," he told me under his breath, "is best, grape second."

The narrower world of fly fishing is not a club unto itself; it has no true rules or guidelines other than those we impose upon ourselves. But those who fish mostly with weighted nymphs, woolly buggers, and streamers sometimes consider those who exclusively prefer dry flies to be snobs; and many a dry-fly fisherman simply finds no connection between his fishing and what a lead-core man does. Debates seem to convince no one.

The visitors to Spring Creek were mostly fishermen who fished only the dry fly or preferred to do so. A few were pretty exclusive about it. One fished only with flies he tied himself, #16 or smaller. He tied beautiful flies, all imitative, and had thought deeply about his fishing. His fishing was such an intense commitment for him that when he came back to the Suburban one day and I asked him lightly, "Have fun?" he replied, "I never have *fun*."

The late Al McClane took his fishing with greater ease. He came to Spring Creek one day before his luggage had arrived at his lodge and fished in a straw hat and tropical sport jacket and shirt, in loafers. A stylish caster and practical fisherman, he went directly to a run of broken water, fished from an upright position that would keep him dry, and had a fine time catching four or five big browns on a Humpy.

Craig Mathews caught a dozen good fish the morning he came, a number of them from truly difficult flat-water sections where I had not yet taken a fish, which he had not fished before. He easily destroyed all the theories I had been collecting except one: an ace fisherman always catches fish.

Datus Proper must have a slanted view of me. The one morning we fished together on Spring Creek we ambled up the East Branch together, he a long lean Jeff to my plump Mutt, catching a few good fish each and talking a lot, never more than a few feet from each other. At one tough bend I spotted a steady rise in a two-foot pocket along the opposite shore, across two currents, into a heavy wind, sixty-five feet by a backhanded double haul upstream. It was an impossible chance so I gave it to him. He looked, said I'd seen the fish first and it was mine. "It's impossible," I muttered, and drew line off the reel coarsely, false cast far upstream, then double-hauled backhanded in the general direction of the cove.

The wind caught the fly and deposited it, with a couple of generous feet of rumpled leader, a foot above the cove. The fly headed downstream, tucked into the cove, the fish came up and took it, and Datus said, "You didn't have to do that on your *first* cast, did you?"

A few times, out of the corner of my eye, I saw visitors fish nymphs and, once, streamers. The culprit sheepishly told me, "I just couldn't resist." But this was rare. Most of the visitors were old friends of Herb's and fully respected the few parameters he put to the fishing. I never found reason to be tempted; the river—with its shallow water and long hatches—was *made* for the dry fly and if you looked it was almost always possible to find rising fish somewhere. Besides, it seemed part of the stewardship of the resource to grant the trout all the water below the surface, to fish a bit less, to key the whole experience to that place where water and air met.

*   *   *

Some of the visitors from England—all advanced fly fishers—
agreed that Spring Creek was more difficult and demanding than
any of the great British chalk streams they had fished. The lack of
cover struck them first, as it had struck me—the absolute need to be
lower than a crouch or even a kneel, the need for constant stealth,
for far fewer back casts, more delicate casts, shrewder imitations.
And all the fish were wild to the core, not stocked. And the water
clarity was so much greater than that of a meadow river in England.
Spring Creek was tougher, less "charming," and filled with much
larger fish. Excellent spawning, a high density of trout foods, year-
round feeding, coupled with a large loss of fish from all the predators and all those undercut banks added up to big fish and easily
spooked fish.

Herb had fished Spring Creek for more than twenty years. He had
fished it every day in June, July, and September, and he had seen it
in all its moods. Sometimes he had learned by looking and fishing
hard, and sometimes merely by walking or driving from one spot to
another he'd happened upon his knowledge: an upside-down brown,
belly-up, taking snails from the bottom of weeds; an eight-pounder
chewing at a dead two-pounder, like a dog a bone; all stages of the
eight or ten hatches on the river; how to fish a particular bend; how
to approach a given pool, when fish could be taken in it, when not;
where certain outsized browns parked (there was always a good fish
along the outer rim of the current at the Car Door Pool), and so very
much more. Once, when we were fishing with Doug Ewing, Herb,
without leaving his seat in the Suburban, told Doug exactly where to
cast in that Car Door Pool, and Doug caught a fat twenty-three-inch
brown on his first cast.

Some of this knowledge I inherited during those first few weeks
at Spring Creek; a little I learned myself, and eventually—despite my

reluctance to accept such a role—I became a kind of local expert, First Guide of the Realm.

The local knowledge I'd acquired was surely more various, less formal, less capable of being articulated than I'd supposed. It was built of instinct, exposure, trial and error, and even the kind of gossip that comes in the form of someone saying he'd seen three fish rising off the point in the South End Pool at 11:15, to a black caddis, #18. And the stomach contents of the few fish Herb killed told stories, too—about nymphs, beetles, riffle beetle larvae, snails, duns, spinners, and the like.

Despite rude lapses, I began to think rather well of myself, especially when visitors came to whom I could explain the hatches, the issues of approach, questions about casting, where the better fish might be found.

In time I had mastered a particularly haunting pool on the Middle Branch. The river pinched into a hundred-yard-long canal-like passage and then made a half turn and opened into a long, broadening, flat stretch, some seventy-five feet across and a hundred and twenty feet long, with a swampy area to the far right, looking upstream, where the river had once gone and now did only partially. The water was clear as glass, over a sand bottom, barely two feet deep, so you could see every fish "on the fin" with startling clarity.

The day I first saw it, as I made my way—rather sloshily—upstream from The Fish Trap, I came within a hundred feet of its tail and saw exactly eleven fish working, all at about the same time, in formation, right up the center of the pool, high on the hog, with heads and dorsals up. Big trout, too. I shivered all over, licked my lips with pleasure, and promptly threw a nice long hard cast right smack down the middle of the pool, putting all eleven fish down in one stroke.

Not so the next time I fished it—when I put them all down on my third cast.

But then I settled down and began to play an expanded version of Vince Marinaro's "Game of Nods." I approached it from the far side and found that the long cast over slack water inevitably caused mischief; from below, I lined the fish; kneeling, from the left-hand bank, I did better, but they went down quite quickly until I sat on a particular tuft of grass and kept my profile and the trajectory of my arm lower. Sitting at that particular point, I could reach the lowest fish and all but one or two of the highest up the run; I made the least possible disturbance and could cast the shortest possible line. In fact, after the sixty-five-foot casts I'd thought I needed when I started to fish the run, the fifteen- to twenty-footers were a shock: they were so much more effective that I made a general rule to the effect that the best cast is always the shortest possible cast.

My flies, already refined, needed further refinement. The very shallow, flat, and open water made the parachutes look like baby chicks. I switched to a comparadun and then to one of Talleur's cut-wing patterns, and then to a pale Cul de Canard emerger. I chose only the comparaduns with the yellowest bodies—having become convinced that the body *does* represent an important feature—and I trimmed the deer hair to only a few bristles, to give it more delicacy. The Mathews Zelon for a tail, or shuck, was generally excellent. And then I refined my arsenal of knowledge even more. On cloudy days I went back to the parachute, in bright sunshine the cut-wing worked better, before the hatch was going good a very sparse Cul de Canard emerger in the film was best.

The knowledge I found was specific to the situation. It was gained not so much by theory but by trial and error, by the infallible test of what drew a trout's rise. It was specific knowledge and yet it bled into more general knowledge, and tried to persuade me that it was fully applicable to general theories of approach, fly design, and fly color. I suspect it was not. I suspect the reason why there is so much dispute among good and serious fly fishermen is simply that their experience is discretely different, that what works here won't work there, that body color is insignificant in one situation, crucial in another.

In the end, after a couple of dozen visits at different times of the day, I did consistently well on this pool. There wasn't a "trick" to it but a world with which I had to become intimate. When I learned a bit more about approaching it properly, and when I got to know more about its bug life, I had also to learn about the size line I could throw over its trout (no heavier than a $\#4$ on calm days, no more than a $\#5$ even in a gale), and the tippet point required—and, oh, a couple of thousand other little matters as well.

In the fullness of time I got a chance to share the pool with an excellent fly fisherman. I knew the guy well and advised him that this stretch might look easy when there were half a dozen or more fish up, but was not. I told him he *must* approach it on all fours, get right to the bank, stay as low as possible, actually sit down, let the pool rest completely, until the fish started up steadily again, and then make the shortest and lowest possible cast to the lowest fish in the run, using a $\#17$ parachute version of the *plat du jour*. His $\#6$ line was too heavy; 5X would look like rope.

He chuckled, thought I was putting him on, and let fly a gorgeous eighty-foot cast across the grass, using a conventionally hackled fly.

Every fish went down on cue.

He tried half a dozen other cute tricks and got nothing.

"You weren't kidding," he said and dropped to all fours, retrieving his line and then holding out his hand for the proper fly. "No, better give me your whole outfit," he said.

You become oddly connected to people when you fish with them. I try to live in the shoes of he who catches fish when I cannot and I try not to act superior to he who blunders, remembering that I have been

there before, many times. I *like* to watch others fish and have been accused several times of meanly hexing the watched, though I watch with only the warmest hope that my neighbor succeed.

Herb, Doug, Mari, and I once came to the big flat above Farrago Pool and found it filled with so many rising fish that it looked like we were in the midst of a hailstorm. Herb told Doug and me to get out and I told Doug to try them; I'd been getting more than my share of fish lately.

Doug fishes a hundred days a year and has fished for salmon, sailfish, and all brands of trout. He's a fine fly fisherman and we became the closest of pals in short order.

My rod was rigged up and I'd put on my waders at the ranch, so I just got out and watched the water. The fish had gone quite berserk. It was the heaviest rise, with the most fish working, I'd ever seen on Spring Creek—or ever did see. The fish were high in the water—snouts and dorsals out; they were wolfing every fly, every Pale Morning Dun, that came down.

Twenty minutes later Mari had set up her camp stool and portable easel and put a large sheet of Arches paper on a board. The fish kept going like mad. The pool had positively exploded.

"What's taking so long?" Herb called from the Suburban.

I told him that Doug was almost ready.

"They're on a binge," said Herb.

I walked around to the back of the Suburban and it was immediately clear to me that Doug was in a state of acute emotional mania. Line was still dropping back through the guides of his rod; his hands shook.

Then his line was through the guides and he couldn't get the tippet through the eye of the fly. Then he did and the knot slipped.

I'd been there, oh, a thousand times before. I wanted to help. I dared not say a word lest I make matters worse. Mari finished a sketch

of "Man Rigging Up," and then another, and then put a third sheet
of paper on the board.

I heard the motor of the Suburban start up, we shut the back door,
and Herb drove off without a word.

Finally Doug had it all together. I was a wreck. Mari later gave
him one of her three sketches and he said it depicted what had been
a glorious moment for him. And of course it *was* a glorious moment—
or, rather, hour: caught in that sweet anxiety of rigging up in front of
a pool full of rising fish is exquisitely exciting for the patsy, impossible
only for those who look on.

Doug's first cast—as would mine have done—put every last one
of those fifty trout down.

One night in late July, a young woman fished a tough pool near The
Fish Trap and could not put down a very large brown for more than
an hour. Gillian, who had once dated one of Herb's fishing friends,
spotted a fish making a terrible commotion near a projecting mound
of grass—no doubt gorging itself on every caddisfly that floated by.
It was a miserable night—raining heavily, bitterly cold, dark early.
Herb and I would not go out in it. We sat in the front of the Suburban
with the heater on, bundled in our heaviest jackets, hands tucked into
pockets, and watched Gillian. Several times I rolled down the wet
window and called out to her, asking her to come in: it was too wet
and cold.

"I think this big one can be caught," she said over her shoulder
and kept casting to that hot corner where the fish kept rising with a
messy, lip-smacking sort of rise.

An hour later she was back, without the fish, and I could see as
she took her boots off that she'd gone in over them. She was soaked
to the skin, so cold she couldn't control her chattering, and furious at
herself for not taking the fish.

"He's still . . . ri . . . sing," she said. "You . . . should . . . try him."

"Not for me," I said.

"Not me," said Herb.

"Maybe I'll go back when I warm up a little," she said.

"No, you won't," said Herb, revving the motor, turning the Suburban toward the north, and heading swiftly for the warm ranch.

8

At the Second Bend Pool

The East Branch, skirting the base of the bench, thick with willows, cattails, and marsh, bore little resemblance to the West Branch or the main stem of Spring Creek. It was a moody, mysterious place. The water was thinner here, and there were fewer bends. In only a run or two, and usually only within inches of the far bank, could you expect to raise a fish on a fly that did not actually imitate a living insect. The fishing was more exacting and the entire attitude of the river here was different, and had a different effect on me.

Herb had not taken me to it for the first ten days, and of course there had been no reason to do so, for we had more than enough fishing elsewhere, especially when the Green Drakes were on. And there was less water here, barely enough for two people to fish comfortably. There was the huge pondlike pool in which we had both taken those large fish, the slick thin head where water from the river flattened and spread; three pools; and then a second huge pondlike pool. Above the second pond, the river grew even more mysterious and wild—and was extremely difficult to fish. I kept saving these East Branch headwaters for a more leisurely day. I kept thinking that some day I'd spend six or seven hours up there, track it to its source, wander a bit and perhaps fish a bit, and see what I could find. Meanwhile, whenever I went up the East Branch, I thought about those headwaters, even as the lower East Branch itself made me strangely contemplative.

One day I caught a marvelous hatch of PMDs where the river went into the first pond, then caddis and PMDs in the First Bend Pool, and more rising fish in the middle run. By 11:00 I'd taken nearly a dozen good trout, all big browns and one twenty-inch rainbow, and had had more than my fill. I'd fished very hard the day before and this burst of action—and success—had bled me of much of my usual ambition. So I decided to sit down on that pleasant inside rim of the Second Bend Pool and merely watch the water.

That great cluster of fish were in the deep hole—thirty or forty of them, in all age classes, and a couple of fish were rising steadily. But I put my rod down in the high grasses and got out a little black notebook I always carry in a vest pocket. Usually I'm too busy to write in it; usually when I'm on the water I want only to fish. But I had been fishing hard, every day for more than three weeks, and I had caught a lot of fish, and I rather wanted to write about those fish I'd found rising in the slick at the head of the pond. I'd had to cast across and slightly downstream to get them and that hour had been exceptionally pleasant. It was best to fish not as I usually did, when I could, but when the fishing would be best—and slowly I had been learning, because of the enormous number of opportunities at Spring Creek, when that best was. The morning had been a revelation; I had not known that the bigger fish, from the pond, would move up during a good PMD hatch, though it was logical that a good head of flies would bring them there. I noted that the first of them had risen at about 10:45, and promised myself I'd come back the next day to see if it was a daily event. I had seen fish move steadily upstream during a hatch, ever closer to the source of a hatch, several times; and I had also seen them, in the big flat, slip back downstream during a heavy hatch, taking flies lower and lower in the pool, using less and less energy and drifting back with the current. I never went to Spring Creek without seeing something new; it was so fecund, so full of chances, that I don't think even Herb had seen all of it, nor would anyone, ever.

A snout came up in the current of the Second Bend Pool but I decided not to pursue it.

I was scribbling rather quickly now.

Learning something new about angling always excites my brain—what would take a specific fish, why it was feeding, how to solve an individual angling problem. I'd done something right and I wanted to understand what. The general laws of angling never held for all situations but they always overlapped. You learned the parts of speech, one at a time, and then you tried to put them all together: not parts anymore, but speech.

There was a "speech" to the writing about fishing, too, and I'd thought hard about its many different languages. Literary friends told me that the great trick was not to use the technical language of fly fishing—the thorax spinners, the 7X leader tippets, the *Hexagenias* and Tricos and PMDs. These, they said, were the jargon of the sport and made it quite unavailable to the intelligent general reader, he who did not fish but read with care and discernment. I'm sure this is so. But the technical language is not the voice of the idiot savant except when it is used by an idiot savant. And I wasn't after a language of literature.

Just as I would not write down, I would not write up. What I was doing, I hoped, with as much skill and invisible artifice as I could muster—as little of the factitious, the posturing as possible—was to report on days afield, and the nature of my relationship to the sport, a relationship that included having, at various times, the keenest possible interest in the minutiae of fly fishing: not using the fancy or occult words, or the Latin, or the names of people and places to impress, but choosing, always, the fullest, most personal way to tell where I'd been. A Trico is a Trico is a Trico; it is not merely a small black fly, nor is it a rose.

I had tried, for more than twenty-five years, to find and to build a language that represented me—something with feeling but not sentimentality, a voice playful but not mannered, not down, not up, not safe, not different just to be different. Some clever populist once wrote to a fishing magazine complaining of the literary references in essays I wrote—to Yeats, Keats, Kafka, and Chaucer—as if these had been laid on with a trowel, with pretensions. He had deliberately misspelled every other word in his letter, feigning a superior ignorance, to defend something called the common man. But I read Yeats and Keats and Kafka in my twenties, on my own, and they changed my life. I wouldn't think of hiding them. They are as much my friends as Len and Mike and Doug; they are as much a part of my speech as Tricos and 7X tippets. Do we read books to get bland pap or mere information or clever nonsense, or to touch another human being? I want those who read me to touch me, to know me—for better or worse—not some studied mask I might put on. And this is the stew of me: Yeats and PMDs, wit that leavens and builds proportion, not sophisticated but (I hope) not dumb, a warm mulch that heats the postmodernist chill. I'd like the stew to be rich enough to catch some of the stillness, complexity, joy, fierce intensity, frustration, practicality, hilarity, fascination, satisfaction that I find in fly fishing. I'd like it to be fun, because fly fishing is fun—not ever so serious and self-conscious that I take it to be either a religion or a way of life, or a source of salvation. I like it passionately but I try to remember what Cezanne once said after a happy day of fishing: he'd had lots of fun, but it "doesn't lead far."

I'd like fish talk to exist not by itself, as a separate estate, but in relationship to scores of other languages that live in me, from art language to street talk to the voices of a thousand writers who echo in my head: not them, nor the echo of them, but something absolutely mine, as real a possession as a Sony Trinitron or a Winston rod or my grandfather's oak dining table.

Perhaps, I thought, sitting on the inside rim of the Second Bend Pool, I am not after trout at all; perhaps this is a ruse; perhaps, among my many ulterior motives, one is the discovery of a language. Or has writing about fishing, which cannot occur without first fishing, become quite as important to me as the act itself? "Wouldn't think of disassociating Fishing from Art," said the happy John Marin—"one and the same thing with me."

A trout shoves its snout up, my heart beats quicker, and I doubt all ulterior motives.

I would as well be here, beside this pool, right now, as anywhere in the universe. I have thought about such a place without knowing it existed. At times I have wished life as simple as this riverbank—the world a logical structure of bend, current, riffle, and pool, the drama already unfolding on the glassy surface, and me, here on the bank, my ass wet, armed with some simple lovely balanced tools and some knowledge, prepared to become part of it for a few moments.

A fish rises with a slight spreading circle; then another comes up, its snout rising from its world up into mine, of air; the drama begins. In a while I may choose to enter it, or I may not, for I have learned enough skills to play; I can cast beyond my shoelaces.

This is a contained, mostly understandable world, and in my nearly sixty years I have understood less rather than more of that other, outside world. Like Kafka, I sometimes seem to hop about bewildered among my fellow men—and they often regard me with deep suspicion. That larger world, away from rivers—and my little place in it—stuns me with its complexity: The old friend who last month looked me in the eye and lied. The other who stole from me. Incrementing details and details. People with Rolodexes for brains. "The beating down of the wise/And great Art beaten down" and down. That bewildering bear I have been—rife with contradictions. The demons in me that demand more of friends than they can ever give, and nothing; that want only solitude like this—and the rush and lights and edge of the cities; that like and crave and despise all "getting and spending."

Tolstoy speaks of an uncle who once told him, when he was a boy, to go into a corner and *not* think about a white bear. I have come to this riverbank, this rarest of corners of the universe, and of course cannot help but think of all that other jazz, and perhaps always will. Pascal says that the trouble with the western world is that we don't know how to be content in an empty room. I am not content here—or anywhere. Nor, as I think of it at the Second Bend Pool, do I want to be content, like a cow or a holy man. I want to put boulders in the way; I don't want to flow without effort. I am restless—therefore I am. And here, now, it's best to get most of it out—like a good sneeze, god-blessed or not.

A muskrat surfaces in the slack shank of the bend, sees me just as I turn and see him—"Since things in motion sooner catch the eye/Than what not stirs"—and, in a lithe gray roll, porpoises and disappears. I follow his wake across the river, into the marsh, up out of the water and into a hole on the opposite bank; he never looks back.

There are more circles and snouts now. I may have been here half an hour or an hour or two hours and the world here feels quite safe from my possible predation. On the glassy surface, a couple of feet from my eyes, I see some flattened spent spinners, two mottled caddis, and half a dozen lovely Pale Morning Duns. I pick out one of the duns

with my eye, one golden speck twenty-five feet out; it reflects the midday sun as it carries on the current and disappears in a rather full and satisfied pecking of the water. The trout here take the duns like that when they get going good. It's unnerving to see them do so. They are as vulnerable now as they'll ever be.

I tie on a parachute PMD, daub it with flotant, strip line off my reel, and make a first tentative cast. But my heart is not in it and the cast is too tentative. I have been thinking too much. The line lands heavily, well short of the nearest rise, and suddenly the pool is perfectly still, as if it contained not a minnow.

Well, I have been snubbed before, by trout and Vreeland, and am sure these fish will come back. Anyway, my brain hasn't quite stopped nibbling on my concentration. And there is no place I'd rather be right now—not Paris, where the fishing is poor; not the beach, where you are asked to take off your clothes in public, put grease on your body, sit in the sand; not the great libraries or concert halls or even the museums I love. This valley feels like home to me right now—me, a city kid, descended from Russian city people, bent always, in a kind of hungry tropism, to space and clear water and open sky.

I would like to be here for weeks, even months, but I could not live all my life in trout country. I have other fish to fry and, difficult as that other world might be, I'd rather be in the thick of it, blasted by its terrors, than sit outside and snipe. If all the year were holidays, to sport would be as tedious as to work—and I have rarely found work tedious. And in the city I can stand before a Rembrandt self-portrait, a Velázquez, a Titian, a delicate Tiepolo, and be in some vital connection with the real thing: not some predigested version of it in a magazine, a reproduction in a book, part of a short course on television, but the real thing. Someone out this way, some years ago, called my Picasso a fraud and wondered how I could teach "Keats, Shelley, and all those weirdos." In my office, things other than trout rise, and some of them "lead far."

Why must I always compare them?

Why, when both are so important to me, must I hold one against the other?

Is it that they always bleed into each other and are never wholly separate?

Or that, looking always for one simple and direct view of this stew of a world, I am tugged in just a few too many directions?

The fish have started to feed again. There are two in the main current, slurping; one dimples in the slack water near the far bank; several are high enough in the water for their dorsals to poke through the slate surface.

I might have been trying for two hours to do something vaguely called "getting in touch with yourself and with nature," but now, with the fish rising freely, I have something specific to do and all that is irrelevant. If I have "gotten in touch" with anything it's the damp bank against which I've been leaning, the grasses soggy from spring seep-age; mostly my elbow and ass, sopping wet, have been in touch.

I watch a teal with a string of five or six ducklings, like a tail, slip up out of the pool and around the bend. I see a couple of killdeer chicks, the size of golf balls, scurry into the underbrush.

The fish are going good now.

I check my fly, draw enough line from my reel, look at the simple happy scene before me, of five or six rising trout—and then calmly tattoo them.

9

Major Tactics

As the days moved on into late July—a string of long bright days, like stones in an Indian necklace, fishing and painting—the fishing changed yet again.

Some of it grew easier. There were grasshoppers in the fields now and it was fun to wade wet, in khakis and sneakers, up the West Branch, casting a Jay-Dave Hopper right up against the far bank and chugging it once or twice. The fish struck explosively. Sometimes, for a fraction of a second, you could see a fish just before it struck—a bright flash of auburn and white, bolting from beneath the undercut banks, angling up and out toward the fly. It sent shocks through me.

And sometimes, when there were grasses but not thistles on the opposite bank, I'd cast onto the shore and tug the fly off, so it dropped with a splat, the way a grasshopper would, coming down out of the grasses.

I found it extremely pleasant to walk up the river on a blistering afternoon, the sun brilliant—opalescent, violet, even through double-strength Polaroids—and the spring water cold and sharp against my legs. There was a happy randomness to grasshopper fishing.

Sometimes, coming along the inside, slack edge of a bend, I'd spook fish from beneath the undercut banks, from no more than six or seven inches of water. At first I thought it a freak that fish of such size would position themselves where the water was so shallow and there was virtually no current to bring them food. I could not remember having read of another river where big trout would make their stand in such places. And these were among the biggest trout in Spring Creek—fish well over twenty-four inches, sometimes at least thirty, broad and very dark, so sure of themselves that they moved slowly and steadily into the deep water in the shank of the bend, fish the size of a muskrat, fish that never failed to shake me silly.

It was natural to fish up the West Branch bends from the slack side, casting to where the current traced the far bank. It was logical for big fish to be under the deeper banks, where food would come in a continuous belt to them, where they were protected from predators by the broken water and had more depth in which to maneuver. And I got many truly fine and large fish from that current line and even from the center current of a bend, where large fish frequently busted up from the depths for a meal as substantial as a grasshopper.

I took two of the largest fish I'd taken from these West Branch bends—from a large pool whose path must have been changing. The water came down a narrow chute and once must have swept off to the right, creating a large half-circle of a pool. Over the years, the far arc of that pool had silted up and vegetation had begun to grow in some sections—all of which forced the current to make its turn more sharply, with less dallying in the far pool. Working my way up toward that bend on a day in late July, about 2:00, I saw several swirls at the surface just where the heavy current hit the slack eddy. There was a defined seam, where the eddy pushed upstream and the headlong current swept down, and the fish was rising smack along that line.

I had been fishing a #16 Elk Hair Caddis in the pool below, where I'd found two fish rising to a tan caddis, but there were no flies in the air—and the size of the surface disturbance suggested a fish feeding on larger fare. Stupidly, I changed to a grasshopper without changing my 6X leader. The fish slammed the big fly on the first cast and I snapped it off at once.

A few minutes later I tied on another hopper, this time on a thick 4X tippet. On my second cast along that seam, in virtually the same spot, a second fish, at least the size of the first, came up, smashed the fly, and bolted directly downstream. It was a powerful brown and I wondered for a moment whether it wasn't the same trout, which might not even have felt that first hopper break quickly in its lip. Even with the heavy leader this time I could not turn it. I had to follow the fish three bends downriver before it slowed and gave in—a bright, brilliant fish, better than two feet long, no sign of my first hopper in its lips.

After kicking out four or five alligators from the inside slack banks, I often stopped well below a pool and fished that unpromising bank with great care. I'd start sometimes at the bottom and fish it a foot or two higher with each cast, but the water was so thin and placid that I spooked the fish before I put a fly over them, and abandoned this scheme. Later, I fished these banks just below the point of the bend, trying to get a long float in that slack water—but I gave that up, also.

In the end, I came to think that those fish were virtually uncatchable, that they might move into the center current to feed on a heavy hatch of a fly as big as the Green Drake, or even to the far bank, but that they did not feed regularly when they were in that spot and could not be caught. Bill Willers, the trout biologist, later told me that he thought such fish might be social rejects—too big and slow to compete with stronger fish along the other bank. I don't know. I only know they scared me silly and I never came close to raising one.

I found other fish that could not be caught—at least not by me—and I liked their presence in the river. They represented a kind of ultimate challenge, a chance for me to grow.

I never caught a fish in the long deep stretches of the upper end of the East Branch. In these mysterious headwaters you could see dozens of truly large trout but I spooked every last one of them before I got within casting distance.

The toughest—and most frustrating—of all spots for me was the exit slick to the Second Pond on the East Branch. Here all the food from the broad pond, several hundred feet across and more lengthwise, funneled down into a slick some forty feet across. The water ran over white sand here and was no more than several inches deep most of the way across. When the larger trout from the pond moved into this area to feed, they were more skittery and paranoid than the Paranoid Pool trout: huge black forms, constantly in motion, wavering back and forth like the shadows of sun through clouds, watching always upstream and, with the merest break of the surface, taking some insect from the top. I could not catch these fish. I did not once come close to catching them. I tried crawling on my belly through thistle and high grasses but when I got to a casting position they were gone. I tried going to a spot and then sitting still as a heron for twenty, then thirty minutes. Yes, the fish came back—and then, as I raised my arm to cast, they'd take flight.

I tried many times to put a fly over them without their scattering first, and always failed. They seemed to me the most difficult trout I'd ever seen and in the night I dreamed of how they might someday be caught: by waiting great lengths of time, until they got to feeding heavily on a substantial hatch; by using a small—perhaps six-foot—rod that cast a smaller shadow, and by casting far above them, so the line never traveled above them; by casting a very loose line, with a great many S curves in it, so the line would not drag. You might have to wait four or five hours, or a day, or two days to get a couple of really good chances. That's the kind of fishing this was—and I was not quite ready for it. I was closer than I had been several weeks earlier, but the Second Pond Slick was miles beyond me.

When I reported all this to Herb he chuckled and said that it became a bit easier when the water was ruffled and the sky overcast—but not much. When the fish got down into the slick they knew how vulnerable they were; they were there to feed, but always with an eye for danger. Herb had taken some fish from the Second Pond Slick—but not many. Doug Ewing, who had gone to pieces when the big flat exploded, had taken the largest fish he'd ever taken on a dry fly—a twenty-nine-inch brown—from the slick.

I got several of the harder trout to rise in other tough places as the last week began: in the Third Bend Pool of the East Branch and even in the Paranoid.

The Third Bend Pool is the first bend below the impossible slick. There is a run of some three hundred yards—narrow and swift—and then the East Branch makes a right-angle turn. Beyond the outer rim of the current there is a slack flat area about eight feet wide by twenty feet long, created where the run bounces off a couple of knots of shrubs. Dermot Wilson liked this pool, Herb told me, and could sit for hours watching it. The fish—one, sometimes two—were in the slack area. You either had to cast directly upstream to them, across flat water, from the left-hand bank—as Dermot did—or, from the right,

across the brisk main current. The logic of fishing from the left side was of course to remove the problem of drag; but the fish were always in the upper end of the slack water and that meant casting across fifteen feet of thin, shallow water. I could not do it with sufficient delicacy and must have put ten free-rising fish down either by lining them or having line and leader fall too heavily on the water behind them, where the slightest movement sent ripples throughout the entire flat area.

I tried from the right but the main current invariably dragged the fly before a trout had a chance to see it—and drag here meant a fish down for half an hour.

Then one day I found a single fish high in the water, wolfing every PMD that came down. You could see its snout come up out of the water and the white of its mouth open widely. The fish was high on the hog and had lost all caution. And, from the shadow it cast on the white sand bottom, it was a perfectly huge fish.

I got so excited that my first cast from the right-hand side was fifteen feet too far and I stopped it abruptly in midair, so that a great clump of loose line fell on the current while, miraculously, the fly and only the leader flipped left of the current and landed a foot above the great trout. Pure serendipity. I could not have duplicated that cast if my life, quite literally, had depended upon my doing so.

I was standing at a spot from which I'd actually made several astonishing casts, none with brilliance aforethought. From that spot I'd cast to the cove thirty feet above the backwater that day with Datus—and raised an impossible fish. I had accepted Datus's compliment of having raised the fish on my first cast, and then, a moment later, had lost the trout.

I did not lose the trout that rose to my miraculous plop cast into the slack water. The fish turned instantly when the fly came over it, took the #17 PMD in a rush, and bolted like a bonefish up the run toward the pond. Shocked, I let it take out all the slack line, got it on the reel, and began to gallop upstream after it, the fish already thirty feet into the backing. I made a tremendous commotion as I turned the corner brusquely, barely keeping the line out of the grass, and stomped noisily up the fast heavy run after the great fish. It never jumped. The fish just went hell-bent for the great pond and never turned, straight up the center of that fast run, with its sharp gradient. Then, in the difficult slick, with ninety feet of fly line, fifty feet of backing, me, and the gradient urging it back, the great fish hesitated for the first time and the current began to tug it back. I reeled madly, let slack line come between me and the fish, saw it slipping downstream in the center of the river toward me, began to strip back line with great ripping motions, lost contact again, regained control, lost control again, and saw the great brown trout slip downriver not two feet from my boots. The fly was still in the corner of its mouth. The fish was three or four inches longer than two feet—and fat as a bass. I'd never had a fish that size take a dry fly.

And then, from below me, it turned and headed up the left bank, going under the bank, coming out, going deeply under again as I put as much pressure on it as I dared. And then it was in a tangle of willow roots. I felt only dead weight. Quickly I waded to the bank, saw it a few feet up into the mass of roots, touched it with the fingers of my right hand, and it was gone.

By fluke or by skill, I was raising more and more of the tougher fish. On the inner rim of the Paranoid Pool—an impossibility within a difficulty—I saw a huge snout rise up and then descend. We were reconnoitering the lower water and I had taken three good fish from the flattest water. I felt up to it.

The fish required a directly upstream cast, through the current that came down between me and the fish. But every time it came up

and I pitched to it that way, I lined the fish and it went down. What to do?

Gently I stepped a few feet to the right, cast directly above me, and then hooked the fly left—and the fish took it in a lurch.

In fact, what began to trouble me now were not the bigger, tougher fish that I did not catch but those that I did not fish for.

There is one that goads and taunts me to this day, a fish I saw from a high ledge on a rock cliff, gazing down into a run I'd never fished it looked so unpromising, though I always fished the pool above it. I was moving upstream to that pool after a morning in which I'd fished rapidly through a few miles of water, and from the forty-five-foot height of the cliff looked down and saw a mammoth fish, high in the water, sipping duns or perhaps floating nymphs. Had I been on the shore, I might not have seen it, for the huge fish barely kissed the surface. But from above, I could see its every movement, even when it chased a few six-inchers and dashed downstream for a few minutes. It always came back to the same spot, which seemed to have no particular features to recommend it: it was just in midwater. The fish was one of Spring Creek's thirty-inchers and it was in one of those rare—most rare—moments of absolute vulnerability.

What I should have done was perfectly obvious: mark the spot clearly in case I could not see the fish from the opposite shore, retreat the few hundred yards I'd just come along the ledge of the cliff, climb down, walk another hundred yards until I could cross, then come up the meadow on the opposite side and fish for this prodigy of nature.

But I was lazy.

It was late in the morning, past lunchtime.

Perhaps I could raise it from this side, from above; clearly it could not be fished from the base of the cliff directly below me.

Perhaps it would be there in the evening.

Or tomorrow morning, when the PMDs were on again.

But when I climbed down the upstream end of the cliff I could not see it again, tried three stupidly careless blind downstream casts, and then one thing led to another and I never saw the fish again.

Not ever.

And I'm made furious at myself every time I think of the entire episode.

One afternoon, the sun at high blaze, Herb asked if I'd like to fish the Back Channel with him. This was a relatively short piece of water, he said, and would take about two hours to fish properly. It was one of the toughest sections on Spring Creek and I had a suspicion he'd saved it until he thought I was ready for it. I was as ready as I'd ever be; we'd be heading East in three days.

After the East and West Branches of Spring Creek come together, the riverbed widens dramatically; in several places, spotted with bars or actual islands, it is three or four hundred feet across. These are the great flats that provide such exacting fishing, large very slow pools where every feeding fish is immediately visible, and where the trout are cautious in the extreme.

The Back Channel runs behind one of these islands, taking a small portion of the main flow and winding it around a twisted island, festooned with wild rose, thistles, and rotted duck blinds.

We started on that bright hot afternoon where the Back Channel sweeps in from the left and enters the main river, fishing up to a deep right-angle bend pool that had one good fish flush in the middle of it, rising steadily in a classic sucking down of the water. As soon as he saw the fish, Herb found some trouble with his equipment, began to fuss with his reel, and insisted I try for the feeding fish.

The Pale Morning Duns were still on and I saw a dozen gold specks, a little flotilla, near the head of the run. By the slow nature of the rise, the deliberate breaking of the surface, it was clear the fish was taking the adult.

From where I had to cast, the distance was ten feet farther than I thought I could manage comfortably, so I begged off, said I'd rather wait and have the pleasure of watching him take the fish. No soap. It was my fish. So I tried a first cast and came down fifteen feet short, and rather hard. I pressed a bit too much and the next few casts collapsed in a heap. Then I double-hauled the line to where the fish was feeding but the line slapped the water and the fish simply stopped feeding. Well, there it was: my old incompetence coming back.

Some of Herb's passion for the most difficult fish, the most interesting fishing challenge, had infected me. I could not get the big one I'd seen from the cliff out of my mind; I kept thinking of the Paranoid and the Second Pond Slick, and every tough chance I'd seen or tried or missed or failed to try. But I had none of Herb's great concentration of power, his precision casting—and I still gave up too easily.

I reeled in slowly, checked my leader and fly, put a bit of flotant on the fly with my fingers, and looked at Herb, who was still fussing with his reel. I did not think the fish would come back. The hot hard glare of the sun must have made it scoot to the bottom, and it would stay there all afternoon.

But in a few minutes the fish was up again. There were simply too many golden bonbons slipping by overhead.

"Show me how to do it, will you?" I called.

"Your fish," he said.

"Are you going to spend the whole afternoon playing with your tackle?"

"I sure the hell hope not. Go on. That fish can be caught."

The fish was rising in exactly the same spot, so I cast again, this time a foot above and to the left. It was a rather miraculous cast for me, I thought, and I was shocked that the fish did not agree. But I tried again, immediately, and made another lovely cast, and again the fly

came down over the fish and he rose an inch or so away and instinc-
tively I struck, ripping the water, putting the fish down again.

"That's it this time," I said.

"I intend to sit here until you catch that fish, Nick."

"I've had my chances."

"The fish can still be caught."

"By me?"

"By you. Take your time. Try another fly—maybe a very sparse
Sparkle Dun. It will take me an hour to clear up this mess in my line."

I wasn't at all sure what he was doing, if anything practical, but
he had his visor off and a little pile of paraphernalia on a rock in front
of him now. I saw ointment and bug dope and several times he applied
each, and then continued to fiddle with his reel or pretended to do so,
and there was nothing to do but pursue this impossible fish. Well, if
there was really no hurry, perhaps I'd just tuck in, take my time, figure
out how to raise this fish, then take it.

I sat down on a little island, got out my fly box, and found a very
sparse Sparkle Dun to replace the parachute I'd been using. When the
determined trout started to feed again, ten minutes later, I cast at once,
then again, the second cast falling just right—above and to the fish's
right, so the fly got a foot and a half of good float before it came
directly over its feeding position.

I leaned forward, tense.

And nothing happened.

"Thought that one was it," Herb said. I did not think he had been
watching me or the fly. "Good cast."

I got three more decent floats, and then made another sloppy cast
and the fish went down.

We'd been at the spot forty-five minutes now. I did not want to
leave until I had hooked the fish. I was determined now to raise it. I
watched the water near the bend carefully and saw a few more PMDs

come down. There were also a few midges on the water, but no caddis. I felt sure that the right fly was a PMD, and that the dun would be best. The five or six different designs had each taken fish for me on both branches at various times, and the Sparkle Dun should have been the right fly. Perhaps there was something about the slant of the sun, the depth of the water here—or whatever—that simply did not allow the few patterns I'd tried to fool this fish. The water was deeper and the bright sun might actually make the surface more opaque. I thought I might try Talleur's cut-wing pattern. It was tied with a very blond body, only a few wisps of hackle, and the cut wings might provide a stronger silhouette here. So I tied one on.

On the first cast, above and to the right, the fly picked up the current, twisted slightly, then rode directly across the still-spreading circles of the trout's last rise and the fish took it in an instant and I smiled with jubilation.

"All right," said Herb, "let's go catch a few fish now."

After that deep bend pool, the Back Channel grew as small and shallow as a small carrier canal on a British chalk stream—perhaps twenty feet across, rarely more than several feet deep, over a light sand bottom. It was immensely difficult fishing and I barely caught one small fish. As soon as you stepped into the water, ripples went out for sixty feet; every cast seemed too hard; and the trout, everywhere, were skittery.

The channel is no more than four or five hundred feet and we were at the remotest section of it an hour later. Together we looked up a hundred-foot stretch of water—narrow here, with a glassy surface, little cover, none of the water more than eighteen inches deep. As we stood beside each other, scanning the water for a feeding fish, I kept thinking how the shallow water meant that the fish had a tiny cone of vision and a fly would have to float within inches of its lie if it were even to see the thing. There were no trees here, nothing to cast shadows, so the full light of the bright blue sky was over the water. Anything moving above the fish would scare them silly.

I took a small tentative step and the ripples and little waves went out forty-five feet ahead of me. I moved an arm and a fish from the far bank darted madly upstream. A very good fish, too.

I was still astounded at how many truly large fish in Spring Creek could be found in some of its smallest, shallowest water.

Ah, the sweet mad toughness of this.

Herb and I stood for five or ten minutes, still as poles, scanning the surface for a dorsal, a wake, a delicate rise. It would have been lunacy to cast without seeing a fish. But there seemed to be none. Herb lit a cigarette and watched the water. I tried not to move a muscle.

Then, where the current hit off a point some seventy-five feet upstream and made a slight but discernible ten-foot foam line, a fish came up with authority. There were still a few PMDs on the water and I had to think that they were what had brought this fellow to lunch. Up he'd come, every minute or so—not much more frequently than that. I imagined him a wise old dog of a trout, fat and territorial, not given to feeding binges any more, having a sweet tooth for these little sulphur bonbons, perhaps a Green Drake or two, always a hopper. The way he lolled just under the surface, dorsal out, and the steady, heavy way he moved, turning as he took a fly, suggested that he might be one of the Spring Creek alligators.

I could not even contemplate the cast necessary to take such a fish. I knew just enough to know that I would botch this one savagely. You could not cast directly over the fish or it would surely bolt for safety. If you cast to the right and hooked the line left—as I'd done for the first trout of the afternoon—the bulk of the line would fall on the shore, in the thistles. If you cast too roughly, by millimeters, no matter where the fly landed the fish would vanish. False casts would be disastrous. The water dropped off toward the left and some brush there would make all but some brand of steeple cast impossible from that side—and such a cast inevitably would come down too hard. And you'd get one cast, no more. The water was too thin, this fish too wary; like a Japanese brush painter, you'd have to catch it just right on the first try or try again some other time, on other paper. You couldn't correct a mistake. It had taken us a couple of hours to work our way around to this spot, I'd be leaving in a few days, and I was sure we wouldn't fish the Back Channel again this trip. Herb said it hadn't been fished in several years.

Five years ago I would not have thought twice about turning such a fish over to the better fisherman. During my first weeks I wouldn't have hesitated to do so. Now I thought twice—remembered my earlier success, my dozens of recent successes—and then decided to turn it over. I was a better caster now, a shrewder tactician, but this was out of my league.

Herb grumbled, I insisted, and then he said all right, he'd try it, and he stripped off a great number of coils of line, quietly, watched the water for five minutes and seemed to be looking for a rhythm in the fish's rises, found what he was looking for, hesitated for another moment, and (with one false cast to the side, over the land) made the most astonishing cast to a trout I've ever seen. I'd seen Herb make some spectacular casts; this transcended them all. As best I can reconstruct what happened—and I have replayed it a dozen times—he cast partially *underhand* (so that the line never rose more than a foot off the surface of the water, and thus could be laid down lightly); he cast far to the *left*, across the stream (so the line never came near the fish); and then he hooked the line back to the right, so that the fly flipped over near the spit of land, several feet above the fish, caught the little line of current exactly, and came down over the place where the riseform had been just a minute before. I should add that there was, when he cast, a brisk downstream wind against us and that the cast was comfortably seventy-five or eighty feet.

It was a magical moment.

I let out an immense gasp of air.

And the fish came up as nice as you please and took the fly.

Later than afternoon I was treated to one more prodigy of technique. We'd come to the beginning of the channel and against the far bank there was a sweeping curve of perhaps 180 degrees—not fast but with a steady foam line that traveled about seventy feet from top to bottom, never more than an inch or two from the bank.

It was a fishy looking spot, with enough depth to hold good fish, and those undercut banks might well harbor something of astounding size. We had alternated fishing the last few runs and I'd just taken a decent fish on a parachute PMD. I'd seen him rising midstream, smack in the middle of a little broken water, and had nailed him on the first cast. The sweeping bend was Herb's pool and I waded carefully to the left bank to sit on the edge of the island and watch.

Tough fishing stretches you, provides you with skills and confidence for a thousand lesser moments—and it eggs you on to take great chances. It's not just courage that's required, of course, but some knowledge of the kinds of major tactics that can be necessary on a trout stream, and then a perfection of the skills needed to enact them.

Herb waded slowly up the silted area, away from the current, until he'd positioned himself where he was able to fish up to the top of the bend. His first cast was a bit short; it picked up the current a few inches from the bank but pulled out into the slack water about five yards downstream. His next cast, though, was perfect: it landed within inches of where the incoming water hit the opposite bank, picked up the current line, and floated downstream flush in the feeding lane. As

it went, Herb manipulated the line so that he fed out an inch or two,
carefully, as the fly headed into the farthest deep bend of the half-
circle, going away from him, still drag-free, and then he took the line
back in trifles as the circle turned and came closer to him. The fly
floated without a trace of drag. When the float had gone twenty feet
I leaned forward to see the bit of gold better; when it had gone forty
feet, still in the foam line, still without drag, I began to hold my breath;
when it had cleared the farthest point of the bend and started to come
back, my chest was knotted with expectation.

But nothing happened.

Herb got two of the next three casts to float like that and I could
not believe no fish came out to take the fly.

None did.

Sometimes they just won't come to play.

10

Time and the Headwaters

The clock began to lose significance by the second week and by the fourth was virtually gone. We were on the water when we thought the flies would start and we stayed until we were hungry or blown off by heavy winds and rain. We returned to the river after we'd eaten in the late afternoon and got back to the ranch well after dark. After a meal of elk roast, morels in cream sauce on chicken, a pheasant Craig had brought over, some mallard breasts, or a slumgullion Herb had made before we came and had frozen, someone might say, "Eleven-thirty," with some half-speculative musing sense of remarkable discovery, and we'd go off to sleep soon afterward.

When we fished the Back Channel, the time was merely however long it took to fish around that bend properly. We wanted to be near the Third Bend Pool or the Horseshoe Bend when the big fly came and at the big pondlike pool at dusk, once the caddis started to hatch. I had learned *sitzfleisch* and could sit at the big pool or the Second Bend Pool for as long as I felt like doing so—for as long as there was a chance to catch fish or learn something worthwhile. I left when I'd seen enough or caught enough or the wind or rain started. Boredom, which is a dumb function of time, figured not at all for me at Spring Creek; I was not bored for an instant, ever, on that river. Tension, a more dramatic function of time, was measured not in duration so much as intensity: a fly floating ever so slowly in the big pool toward a delicately rising trout, sweeping slightly left with the wind, sailing without drag as I inched out line and leaned dangerously forward, shocked me with the power of the tension it built—though in clock-time the event took seconds.

I became more concerned with *thingness* than *whenness*. I found less and less imperative to create and live within a category of time. I thought only about the number of days remaining before we'd leave.

Two days before our flight east, Herb took a visitor up toward the south end of the West Branch and I decided to walk alone, far up the mysterious East Branch, toward the headwaters.

I had been up the swampy upper East Branch several times, once with Herb, once with Jim Bowman, and both times had found some fish. But we had talked a lot both times and had not fished hard, and I had gotten barely a hint of the place and a story about one guest who had once caught a thirty-inch brown that must have stayed up after spawning, a report about how Herb's ranch managers, when they were young, had trapped up in that small water and how one had been bitten by an otter, and some admonitions from Herb about how dangerous the swampier sections could be. There was a mysterious quality to the entire upper East Branch and as I stuffed some elk sticks and a bar of cheese into my vest and headed toward that section I felt a great sense of expectation.

The headwaters of all spring creeks are pellucid, alive; I've been told that a strange vitality, a wildness, thrives in such places, that headwaters are numinous. For Spring Creek they were the source—not a single place but hundreds of upwellings, coming from hillsides as well as the low places in the fields. I found a dozen such springs on my way up—white sand on their floors, barely a hint of the movement of water coming up and oozing down, in slow rivulets, to the main river. Some of them had newly hatched fry; others were perfectly still, alive but without movement.

A lot of people have been tracking rivers to their sources lately; if not an epidemic—but if so, benign—it's surely a desire to find some further meaning in all this sloshing around in streams. People seem to be saying, "There must be more to it than the catching of fish—and perhaps those meanings are to be found in the headwaters."

I went to the headwaters that day in late July, on next to my last day of fishing, to find trout. I thought there might be a few old soaks up there, fish that, like the big one Herb had mentioned, had gone up to spawn in the fall and stayed. I thought the fishing might be different, too, from the larger water I had been fishing so hard. Part of what we do on rivers is follow our nose. We want to see more. I knew just enough about this water to be curious to know more.

As I left the main river for its East Branch and followed it a mile or more upstream, beneath the bench, it grew narrower and deeper, the water increasingly small and bright and quick. Water seeped into the main current from more and more springs and all seemed wilder, fresher.

Now and again I stopped and tried to make myself very still. Stillness calls forth stillness. You have to seek such stillness consciously, I think—the movement of not one muscle of your body, the making of yourself into some kind of receptacle to be filled up by whatever is out there. In my youth I read the mystics—Madame Blavatsky, Walter Hilton, Evelyn Underhill, Sri Ramakrishna, Baron von Hügel, Zen masters, saints, searchers, and finders—and wanted to be one with what was out there, whatever that was. You knew it that way, they said. You became what you touched, what you led to an "I = Thou" relationship, what you saw.

An awful lot of garbage comes in this way, and it rather hurts to "become" some old friend who looks you in the eye and lies, betrays you, then walks away. So I thought I'd become the water and the trout and the heron and the Pale Morning Dun. At my size it became difficult to become a Pale Morning Dun, though I'm told that in time a man may bugger a flea, so gradually I just made a pleasant experience of being in the natural world, and that day, up in the headwaters, I tried to summon up that old stillness I sought. My ears grew keen to a dozen sounds—the light movement of the river, the pop or sucking sound of a rising trout, the fall of spring water, seeping down the bench, into the cattail bogs, and dropping from a high bank into the stream, in a miniature waterfall that I found and watched, for no good reason. I heard the peep and my eye caught the killdeer family in the high grasses; when a blackbird dive-bombed me, I looked around and found its nest in some high shore grasses, near a stand of wild iris, with four chirping newborns, beaks open and beckoning. I spooked a heron and it lifted off with a heavy whirr of its huge wings. A lithe otter popped its head out near an undercut bank, porpoised, and disappeared. A mother mallard saw me, beat the water with her wings, and then glided upstream, away from the chicks I was not supposed to see huddled in some overhanging grasses. I sat for twenty minutes—or was it an hour?—near one bend pool some thirty-five feet across, slick, with a sand bottom, and, at first, not a fish

in sight. I wondered if that was a fish under the far willow shrub or a downed willow branch, whether I was wasting good fishing time looking at killdeer and ducklings, whether I should stay or go.

It was very quiet up here in the headwaters; nothing tugged at me but a world happily, electrically about its own affairs. Quiet was the ante to enter. No voice, sound, horn, bell called. Degas, seeing a telephone for the first time at his friend Forain's house, said: "So that's what a telephone is . . . one rings for you and you come running."

I pulled line off my reel and made a brief cast across the stream. Instantly the water was a hive of darting fish. Five, six, seven of them—several quite large. Where had they been? I'd have to look harder, approach and cast with far greater stealth, if I wanted to catch—or even see—any of these headwaters' trout. Everything here was hooked to everything else. The slightest movement alerted every living creature. A raised arm and forward cast meant a circus of wraithlike forms, all aquiver.

A mile farther upriver and I came to a sharp bend, 120 degrees, where the small river hit up against a soggy bank, formed a slow backwater now half-filled with waterweed, and then scampered downstream. It was a moody, lonely backwater, and I knew it must hold fish—and that I could come a lot closer to them because of the depth and broken surface. So I pitched a cut-wing Pale Morning Dun up into the entering riffle, followed it several feet, and then struck firmly to a rise. The heavy fish took me directly into the weedbed and broke me off. Another, two casts later, did the same thing. I shook a little, sat down to tie on a new fly, and then, from the sitting position, cast again. For a third time a good fish struck at once, let me feel its weight in the belly of the pool, and then went into the weeds. I had seen none of the fish, only felt them. That way they may have seemed larger than they were. They felt very large.

That was enough here so I went on upstream, my legs a little tentative, where the water grew still smaller and the surrounding land became more of a bog. The land here was honeycombed with muskrat holes and softened with spring seepage. Everywhere I stepped I sank in; the banks were undercut ten or even twenty feet in places, and the land oozed with clear spring water. When I approached any marshy bend I had the feeling that there were trout in front of me, behind me, beneath the soggy land under my feet, everywhere but up.

I could not get within thirty feet of the banks of these crystalline pools and runs without seeing those long gray furtive forms jet upstream and out of sight. If they didn't hear my vibrations, they soon saw me—long before I saw them. By the time I got close enough to the river to look into it, trout—some of them well over two feet long—began to dart back and forth wildly.

I felt dumb and clumsy as a slug.

Herb had told me to be wary of the swamp—if not downright spooked by it, as Nick Adams was. But I boldly plunged upstream, sometimes keeping my eyes on the land in front of me, sometimes looking off to the river for feeding fish. "I'm not afraid of the swamp," I thought, and promptly fell a couple of feet into a muskrat hole, up to my waist, smashing my right hand down on a thistle bush. If this was becoming "one" with the natural world, I'd rather, like S. J. Perelman, be "two with nature." But I only got muddy and nearly lost a hip boot. It took me no more than fifteen minutes to get the little thorns out of my palm, and then I was up and looking again.

The only way to take fish like these, in places like this, would be to enter the streambed itself, find a spot near a willow to park yourself, and stand quite still like a heron for a half hour, an hour, unblinking, until the fish regained their sense of security. And then you'd get one cast. Maybe.

Perhaps one day, some year, I'd do that. I didn't have the patience for it that day alone in the headwaters. I wanted to see a lot of this upper section. I'd sat and waited and tried to become one with the muskrat and the crane, and now I thought I'd enjoy covering a lot of territory better.

I marched upriver now, far beyond where I'd ever gone before, anxious to see quite how far I could go, and at last I came to water that would have been much too small to fish with much pleasure. The river had divided a few times and I might have taken one of its smaller tributaries, but I don't think so; I think I was on the largest and it just was not interesting water to me. I'd seen a lot of the smaller springs; it did not mean much to me to find the highest of all springs, the numinous fountainhead of this one branch of Spring Creek.

There might be a decent fish or two in such water, a fish that might be pounded up from an undercut bank on a grasshopper, on a day when there wasn't much sun and perhaps just the right amount of wind; but I didn't feel much like that kind of fishing, either. Fishing was the axial line, the pirn around which all my interest in the natural world spun. I had come to catch a few trout and I simply had not done so yet; so I dropped back, giving the river a wide berth, watching where I put my feet, until I saw a spot that I had marked as promising on my way up.

Here the water ran in a ten-foot band of current along an over-hung bank. The run had a nice chop to it and there was a little mound of grass that I could sit on, thirty-five feet away, low enough not to bother the fish, protected by some slack water and that nice roll of the current. The run might have been sixty or seventy feet long. It bounced against the far bank and then, at the bottom, against a promontory, which led it to turn sharply left and open into a broad slick pool, positively loaded with uncatchable trout, of the stripe I'd been seeing all day. I'd spooked every last one of the trout in the pool on the way upriver.

But the run was different. It advertised its catchable trout boldly, and I was ready to buy a few.

Some Pale Morning Duns were coming down and I watched the little golden sailboats that I'd grown to love so deeply flutter above the water, alight, lift off, or float down on the riffle. A trout rose in a spurt rise in midcurrent. Another rose quietly along the opposite bank, in a two-foot backwater, and another in the far edge of the main current, and one in the tail of the run.

It was a very pleasant spot and I was tired from so much walking and failing and falling, so I watched for a while, saw the fish come up more than a dozen times, and then tied on a thorax PMD. I tied it on slowly and then tested the knot slowly, two or three times. I was in no hurry now. I was as far into the headwaters as I wanted to be and I had found some fish that meant business.

I knew no one had fished up here for several years. It was a happy, private, comfortable, wild spot and I thought it would surely prove a generous spot. I needed just a bit more generosity up here in the headwaters.

I waited still a few more moments, then cast to the head of the nearest seam of current. A golden speck came down with another golden speck an inch or two from it. I leaned forward to see which was which. They looked about the same but then the real one fluttered a few inches upstream, my fly floated well and far—as dry flies will on a little chop—and then a trout rose and took my fly.

It was a strong fish but had nowhere to hide or cause much mischief and I had him six or seven minutes later. Then the river was quiet for a while and I leaned back against a hummock soggy from seepage and watched a lady teal with a string of five ducklings scurry around the bend when they saw me. Now my eyes and ears—wide with wonder, feverishly alive—caught everything: the vole in the grasses, the sandhill cranes near the next bend, the oiled glide of a muskrat. But mostly I watched the water and listened to the water. It was liquid quartz here, over gravel and sand—amber, amethyst, peridot. I felt very close to it. I let the wet ripple of it sink into me, stilling some odd thoughts about the buzz and clatter and tooth of the world, which always tracks me, even here, watching the circles, the slight flag of a dorsal fin under drooping grass, the delicate bulge and lump of nervous water, wildly exciting to me.

In a few more minutes the fish were rising steadily again and I caught the one I wanted on the third float of my fly over it. Then I caught the one against the far bank; and a half hour later, still not having moved, I got the one in the tail of the pool to come up—but I just pricked it and it was off. I lose far too many fish on the downstream cast for there not to be some hooking principle at work, perhaps the position of the hook. But I didn't want to think about that.

I thought instead, briefly, that I could do anything, was capable of any great feat; and at once I worried that I might soon degenerate, with such thinking, into a big-fish fisherman or a Person of Style; and then I realized that of course I was saved from this by the way I would surely continue to dress and a propensity not only for pissing on apples but (as Herb is never shy of reminding me) for admitting same in public.

I'd had a perfectly lovely hour—or was it five, or five minutes?— at that run and, having eaten my elk sticks and cheese a good while earlier, I suddenly felt very hungry.

This is as good a reason as any for a big man to leave the headwaters.

11

Ghostlier Demarcations

During the last three or four days there were steady hatches of caddis at dusk and we fished the first large pondlike pool on the East Branch almost exclusively in the evenings.

Weeds were forming everywhere in the river now and it became more and more difficult to find runnels between them where you could fish. Patches of weed had begun to form on the pond, too—along the far side and upstream on our side—and a fight such as Herb had had with his three-foot trout would have been quite impossible.

The pond was quieter now, tinged with an odd mixture of melancholy, even desperation, as if it were trying to keep its own, not be led down other paths, and I found such feelings in myself, too. Though we had kept no trout from the pond, we had caught or pricked thirty-five or forty fish, and the number of fish showing had diminished. Those that rose seemed to do so with more caution and deliberation.

But after Herb and I had driven to the Farrago Pool, past the Paranoid, up to the South End Pool and the Great Horseshoe Bend, and had fished a bit and talked and looked a lot, we always ended the day, those last days, at the pond.

I mostly took up my favorite position, sitting on a hummock facing out and slightly upstream. There were tan caddis with very long antennae in the air every evening and we'd usually see a fish or two working along the far bank.

One evening, as the sun was dropping low beyond the hills to the west, brilliantly white, a pair of sandhills flew by, squawking, and Herb said he'd seen a couple of good fish near the weedbeds on the far side. From my hummock, I saw him walk downstream to the tail of the pond, where it was shallow enough to ford in hip waders, and head slowly across to that opposite bank to fish for those few trout that were rising. The bench came down close to the water here so you had to use a kind of steeple cast or had to cast from downstream up or roll cast. Even then, the weeds along that entire bank came close to the shore and Herb had to cast over them, which looked neither comfortable nor pleasant.

I watched from my hummock for twenty minutes as he worked his way into position, made a few ineffective casts, grumbled, and fussed with his line, to which strands of weed now dangled.

To the west, the sun had slipped a fraction beneath the rim of the mountain range and the clouds were turning pink.

I saw a bit of nervous water directly above me, among the weeds, but judged it a fish after nymphs. Out more than a hundred feet a

couple of good fish were high in the water, wolfing caddisflies, but they were in a little channel of current caused by the bloom of weed and probably would not move out of it. A huge wake appeared forty feet out, raced downstream, then up, then disappeared—a fish chasing nymphs in open water.

Herb took one good fish, then settled back and watched the water.

I didn't have a shot at a feeding fish for twenty minutes so I finally got up—my pants wet from the soggy hummock—and headed for the slick at the tail of the pool. Herb had crossed more than a half hour earlier and, from my hummock, I had seen four or five very visible and large spreading circles in the slick.

As I rose and, walking well back from the pool, headed west, toward the tail, I watched the pink of the sunset insinuate itself across the sky. The sun was almost gone now and the temperature dropped abruptly. The light, suddenly, was opalescent; the water had become an odd shifting panoply of gray, slate, and black. At times I could see the golden speck of one last PMD a hundred and fifty feet away; a moment later, I could not see a fly twenty feet from the bank.

It was a strange time in this dying and shifting light and I half thought I'd just watch it. I'd caught a lot of fish during the past month, a remarkable month. I was not tired of catching fish but I did not have any urgency to catch them that night. I rather enjoyed not having to catch them.

At dusk, in the slick at the lower end of the big pool, the water was quick and smooth and I could watch the trout ranging back and forth, taking insects that sometimes I could see, sometimes not. With their shifting positions and the slickness of the water, I thought at once that these trout would be as difficult to catch as those in the pinched egress from the Second Pond on the East Branch, where I had never taken a fish. I'd never caught a fish in this slick either and on this next-to-last evening before I left, I thought I'd make my stand here.

The evening was very quiet now. The pink was turning to gray, the temperature had dropped another degree or two. I thought of Stevens's "The Idea of Order at Key West," with its haunting evocation of that magical time when the "ghostlier demarcations" of dusk and art and life breed "keener sounds." I sat on the bank, recited a dozen lines of that poem to myself, and waited for a few fish I'd spooked to come back. I checked fly and leader. I felt poised, alert. A fish came for a big caddis twisting on the surface and took the fly with its lips high out of the water.

I cast above the spot with pretty good accuracy and the Elk Hair Caddis came down directly over where the fish had risen, there was no rise, and then the fly dragged.

I could not see the fish themselves—only their wakes or the neat curl of the surface when they rose—and their positions shifted constantly. They must have been very much like those fish from the pinched neck of the Second Pond. Those fish, which we could see, were wraiths, phantoms—quick shadows in the thin clear water over white sand and small rocks. These fish, like those, must have come into the slick to feed, recognizing that all the food from the large pond funneled into the area. In the daylight, in the upper neck, the fish would know they were fully exposed to all their predators from above, visible in the thin water and against the light-colored bottom. If they became too preoccupied with food, which was why they'd come here, they'd lose their skins.

I looked up to the rim of the bench and saw several antelope silhouetted; in the distance, a coyote, then another, wailed. Those antelope fawns I'd seen the first few days I'd been here would be safe from coyotes by now—or dead. They were up and running within days, but any with the slightest defect would have already been caught and eaten.

Looking up at the rim of the bench I could see tens of thousands of caddis, high and whirling, in mass flight, against the lighter gray of the sky.

The fish came even higher in the water now, less cautious, and I got a good cast up at the rim of the slick and it came down next to another caddis, there then not there in the half light.

I leaned forward, trying to follow them both, trying to keep the real distinct from the unreal.

A fish rose.

No. It was to the natural.

Another.

Yes.

And I had it on.

On the last night we were quiet in the Suburban as it rattled across the benches, down toward the river. The day had been bright, then overcast. It was raining lightly and it was cool, and I thought with this last night as another occasion for hope that this would be a proper chord on which to bring down the curtain.

We came down the last bench and headed off to the right, past the Paranoid Pool toward the Farrago. The water was ruffled from the wind and slate-colored. In the big flat we saw one little splash that led us to stop and watch for a few minutes. There were no more rises and Herb said, "Not exactly a feeding frenzy," as he turned the clanking key chain and headed for the pond.

When we got there he positioned the Suburban so he could look out comfortably and said it did not seem very promising. He'd wait until there was a fish to cast to.

I went to my hummock and hunched over in my slicker against

the rain. The rain was not heavy but it was steady—and the air was cold. Looking out, I could not always tell whether or not there were some rises mixed in with the circles the raindrops made, so I cast several times, then began to cast more frenetically and kept this up for a half hour—stupidly, desperately, not wanting the month to end quite like this, in the rain, fishless.

Once a huge fish—the size of a salmon—leaped, chasing caddis, shaking wildly, pumping adrenalin through me.

I sat for another half hour, then longer. It was dark and very cold now and I could feel the cold working its way through to my bones. In several bursts of some odd compulsion, I cast eight or ten times and then stopped. It was hopeless. I said ten more casts and I'd give it up and counted off the casts audibly to myself.

And then I stood up, took down my rod, and, without taking off waders or slicker, got into the front seat next to Herb and we began the bumpy drive to the ranch.

Up the last bench we went, in four-wheel drive, then along the twisting, rutted road, rain pelting the big tan Suburban now.

"Not a whole lot of action," said Herb.

"I'd hoped to get one last good fish," I said.

"You got plenty of good fish," he said.

"I didn't believe there were so many big trout—or interesting trout—anywhere in the world."

We rattled slowly up the last two benches and then curved at the crest of the last and headed down toward the lights of the ranch.

12

One Last Tough Trout

For five or six years after my first halcyon visit to Spring Creek, I returned for several weeks or so, always in June and extending through the Fourth and on into the bright hot days of July. Three times the river, if that was possible, was more generous. We caught a gigantic Green Drake hatch one year that had us backing away, watching, before it was half over. Herb performed more of his prodigious feats, effortlessly, and I gradually became a steady, resourceful, more consistent spring creek fisherman.

Each year the nearby town held its Fourth of July celebration, with floats and a rodeo, firecrackers and flag waving. Herb and I never went. We stayed close to the river and what celebration we had related to the pursuit and capture of specific fish—days with their own pace, slow and full, with their own bold firecrackers.

"You really ought to come, you know," Mari said of the town celebration, telling us how unique it was—innocent and old and honest. "You and Herbert are old stick-in-the-muds."

Perhaps. But the fishing was too compelling to leave and even a slow day of fishing Spring Creek was more exciting and significant to me than just about anything else I might find in the civilized world, and rarer. When I got near Spring Creek I wanted to be fishing it.

New Junes came and we'd pack up tackle and art supplies and mostly a few plain clothes, and head west—starting at a crowded eastern airport, transferring at Denver, taking a smaller plane to an airport where I might well know three or four people of the few dozen that constituted its crowd, where Herb and Pat—with smiles—were always waiting. The years blurred. Had we caught that remarkable Green Drake hatch on the middle water three or four years ago? Which years did Al McClane come? Was it two years ago that I caught the fat rainbow in the Farrago Pool? Have I mixed some of those other years into that first, miraculous visit, when so much of my fishing life changed? Probably. I've probably done that. And why not? Spring Creek—all its years in one pot—has seemed to me an event separable from all other events in my life. It was always there. It was always a thing in my head, capable of being summoned at any time of the year, capable of sustaining and healing me. Surely it changed. The island in the Paranoid Pool might be smaller, the Great Horseshoe Bend might be cold one year. The pelicans—swooping in formation across a pool—might have skimmed a dozen fish out of the South End Pool. The Nursery might be even hotter than ever, but the flats above Farrago Pool had just as many wild, furtive, darting shadows over the light ochre bottom as it ever had, and I was as hard-pressed to catch them as before, and the channels might be different and the curlew might not stop on their migration from somewhere south up to Alaska, but the smell of mint at The Fish Trap was the same. Old green patches near broad oxbows showed that the river had clearly changed its course over the years, and would continue to do so, as silt accumulated at certain bends and eventually became solid. I never spotted that great fish I'd seen from the cliff again, nor any fish, ever again, in that run, and that goaded me every time I thought of that huge fish free rising. And Herb never failed to rag me about the apple trees growing near the Paranoid Pool.

One winter during those years Herb took ill, and I wondered (as he may have done) whether he would fish again. But he did—his cast as low and powerful and accurate as before, with perhaps only some greater reserve toward the longer treks.

Then a year ago I could not come in June; I traveled to other parts of the world for other purposes, grew heavier still and a little older and a little more tense, and finally arranged for an early-September visit instead, hooked to a business trip to Denver. The time was new for me and Herb had written that a particularly severe winter had taken a toll. Some spots, once good, were barren—skinned, perhaps, by that troop of pelicans we'd first seen two years earlier. Hatches had been sparse all year—with only a handful of Pale Morning Duns and no Green Drakes whatsoever. In September the hatches might be sparser still.

But I felt the same extraordinary sense of expectation as we climbed the first bench, rattled along the familiar dirt road, paused briefly at the last bench to look down at Herb's wealth of waters, that gorgeous blue ribbon laid out casually in the valley.

I noticed, that first day, that the carcass of the calf struck by lightning was little more than a spot now; it made me think of the passage of time since I had first visited Spring Creek, though still not

of Alexander in his tent, Montaigne in his tower, and Saint Theresa
in her wild lament. Perhaps fishermen live in a more temporal world.
At least this one does, at least in his fishing life.

Along the river we found no Pale Morning Duns, few caddis, and
only a modest Trico hatch the first few days. I fished poorly—casting
hard, lining the fish, reverting to tics and glitches I thought I'd lost half
a dozen years earlier. Several times Herb said, "I've never seen you do
that before." I couldn't quite account for the regression. A bit more
weight? A trying year? Business nibbling at my nervous system? An
old friend and teacher who now teaches me how to hate, new ambiguities in a world speeding much too fast for an old fellow who still
types on an Underwood Standard, Model S, vintage 1945.

I fished poorly and my chest grew tense and several times I had
to switch from the demanding flat water to broken water, which was
always far more generous.

Herb stayed in the car more, too.

I caught half a dozen truly fine fish during the week, often in spots
that hadn't fished well before, and several on grasshoppers, banged
rudely against the opposite shore of the West Branch bends.

On the last day I still felt restless, as if this river, which had for
so many years been balm and salvation, was no longer capable of
providing such munificence, perhaps because I had lost some of my
innocent attachment to it or expected it to be more than it was, or
perhaps simply because the world was, this year, much too much
with me.

On the last morning I went out alone, with Mari, and decided to
fish the East Branch. It was a gray day, with a chill and a few dashes
of rain. There had been some Baetis on the water—a #20 dark-olive
fly—and I thought of the jingle, "The worse the weather, the better
the Baetis." We'd seen a few up at the South End Pool the day before
but only one fish had come up, twice, tentatively, and Herb and I had
noted together that this was not precisely a feeding frenzy.

When Mari had set up her folding chair and had taken out the last of her sketchbooks, I kissed her, admonished her to keep warm, and headed off to the left. An hour later I could see the Second Bend Pool, which I had not fished for more than a year. You become attached to pools; something in their attitude or conformation draws forth something in you, or you find an objective correlative for something in you in it. Certain pools talk to you, others don't. Some pools are generous to a particular fisherman but resist all of a much more skillful angler's efforts.

I loved the Second Bend Pool.

I had always done well here.

I had been waiting all week to fish it.

As I approached it, I could see upriver forty or fifty yards, just below the bend itself, three fish rising steadily. The water came around the bend, flattened, and then pinched and came downhill toward me in a pitched gradient, a rush. The fish were in the flat water, lunching.

I crossed to the left, the inside, bank and waded slowly toward my spot. I didn't think my wading would disturb the fish because I was in the heavy water, but I moved methodically, shuffling, keeping my eyes on the spreading circles in the flat water above me.

The fish were happy—rising in that leisurely, steady way that suggests they've put aside all worries, are interested only in the bonbons sliding toward their stations. I saw no flies in the air but in a backwater I scooped up Trico duns, Trico spinners, a couple of caddis—one tan, one mottled—and a few small dark olives, #20. There wasn't a profusion of any of them but one or more were providing an ample picnic for these trout.

When I reached my spot on the inside rim of the bend, I sat down. I was more and more impressed over the years by how sitting kept you lower than kneeling, and the trout in Spring Creek liked nothing less than a figure popping up from their accustomed shoreline, unless it was a white shirt. Then I pulled all the leader and some line through the tip-top, pulled twenty-five feet of line off the reel, and checked my fly. It was a mottled caddis with a little Zelon tail, #16, tied by Craig Mathews, and I thought it would do as well to start with this as with anything else.

When I raised my arm and rod to cast, two fish went down and, for the next hour, never came back. A better fish, farther out, just at the edge of the far current and the flat water, kept poking its snout out; I pitched a first cast to it, the cast was pretty sound, and the fly came down right over the vortex of the fish's rise—and the fish, instead of taking, headed for left field.

"Just what I need today," I said just audibly.

Well, I'd had a fair shot at what looked like a very good fish and, as I'd done too often this past week, I'd messed it up royally. My rhythm was clearly still off. I'd been rushing around a lot this year again, in big gray cities, and had worked long hours the last weekend to get some piles of work done so I could make this trip, which I'd been looking forward to, sorely. On that first day with Herb, I'd put down half a dozen fish that were on Trico spinners; fishing directly upstream to them, I had overcast, lined them, missed their feeding lanes and rhythms, slapped the water—all. I figured that I could make up for all this nonsense on the second day, when I got my bearings. But the second day the Tricos didn't show. Nor did the caddis. Oh, I got a few good fish—one huge rainbow on a Baetis; three on hoppers, fished boldly against some undercut banks; a couple on this little mottled caddis, when I saw a few fluttering near a bit of choppy water I knew had good fish. The river was all right. It had fewer hatches this year but its water and its trout were never healthier. Mostly, I was fishing like a klutz, missing easy as well as hard chances, and I could not seem to get a fix on why.

You look at yourself in hours like that, hard, and you look at your world. You begin to equate fly fishing with your emotional life and your business life, though I'm not at all sure there's any absolute connection. Still, you think some general jaundice in you is causing the yellow in the fishing and you think that fishing better will settle your nerves, or at least become evidence that you've solved the other matters. Maybe that's so. Fly fishing certainly presents itself to the mind at times as therapeutic and coherent and spiritual and capable of being affected by and affecting all else in one's life. Mostly, thinking all these heavy thoughts on the inside rim of the Second Bend Pool, I just wanted to be fishing a little better, with more care, and I felt jumpy, impatient, and the mix was very unsatisfactory.

I had begun this last day of my visit to Spring Creek by wrecking the First Bend Pool with four consecutive sloppy casts; I had pounded up a fish on a Humpy in an upstream riffle; I had tossed a grasshopper against a couple of banks without much enthusiasm; and then, as I watched rain clouds gather to the south, I'd promptly put down three good fish in the pool I'd been waiting a week to fish.

What to do?

I had a couple hours before lunch, and I could stretch these into three if I chose, if the fishing warranted. I'd also have the afternoon, if the rain held off, and early evening. There was plenty of time. There was no reason to feel rushed, though I did.

Perhaps I should walk upstream another half mile or so until I found some more feeding fish; I hadn't been to the headwaters this trip. Perhaps I should fish a hopper hard, match my mood, settle for that; the sun had vanished already but the wind would blow them around—and hoppers were always fun. I liked their rough-hewn quality, the slashing strikes they drew, the fact that they often pounded up very good fish in this river. They were often a satisfying antidote to the very difficult business of fishing a small dry fly on glass-flat water.

In ten minutes I started to get up, noticed that the better fish had begun to stick its head up again, and sat right back down. I continued to watch and he stuck it up above the surface a couple of times, regularly, every fourteen or fifteen seconds, rising in a tight pattern no wider than a square foot. I remembered Herb saying, years earlier, "That fish can be caught."

So I tried him again and this time managed to send five floats over him before he went down.

Perhaps he wasn't on the caddis.

When the trout came up again, fifteen minutes later, I tried first a Trico dun and then a Trico spinner. I was casting with a bit more of a snake in my line now and that enabled me to put the fly a full foot and a half above the snout, exactly where I wanted it, and to have it float two feet below the fish before the fly dragged and I began to ease it toward me. Lengthening my leader tippet by a foot helped, too.

But this tough old evil trout was not munching Tricos. And I soon found out that he didn't much care for the tan caddis, either, even when I changed my entire tippet again, making it still six inches longer. Was he being particularly snobby or did he simply have his own agenda and want to keep his skin?

And then I slapped the water a bit hard with the line and the fish made a terrific swirl and fuss at the surface and disappeared.

That did it, I thought. Gone. For the next week, minimum. I was ready for the hopper.

But for some reason I decided to wait, to play out this hand however long it took. I sat and fussed with my leader; I greased the braided butt slowly so that it would not spritz on the surface, and I tied on still a longer tippet, remaking the knot twice. I watched the place where the bend riffle became flat and I kept glancing down at the slack water near my inside perch, looking for new insects.

Sure enough, fifteen minutes later, the old fellow was back, pressing his snout up as boldly as ever, thumbing his nose at me. Or perhaps he just couldn't help eating, an itch I knew well. The sky was darker now, the wind chilly, and the worse weather made me think the Baetis might get stronger. So I rummaged in my busy vest and came up with a little tin box of #20 dark-olive Sparkle Duns. Well, that would round out everything I'd seen on the water, anyway.

On my first cast with the dark olive, the fly lit, floated a foot, came into the area in which the fish was feeding, hesitated, and then the snout came up, swirled—to my fly or a real one next to it?—I struck, and the fish bolted upstream in a manic rush. I raised the rod high, wound hard to get the fish on the reel, and then stood and high-stepped upstream as the fish headed around the bend and into the heavy run that led into it.

It was a long fight, with edgy moments as the fish went farther upriver, then sulked in the belly of the pool, then made—too late—a few runs below me. The 6X held, the fish began to tire. I backed toward my spot on the bank, sat down, and eased the great fish closer.

When he was in the water near my legs, and turned slightly on his side, I put my rod down quickly—in a clumsy, stupid movement—cupped both hands under the great fish, and scooped him onto the grass. Next to my rod, flapping feebly, the fish astounded me with his girth and length. He was a broad, heavy old fish, in perfect condition; his mouth showed no evidence that he had ever been hooked before. Then I had him back in the water, cupping his belly and holding his tail, and I watched the bright spots on his flanks disappear as he righted himself, and I saw the gills work hard and then regularly. After I'd taken my hands from him, he hung around in the slack shallow water for five minutes, as if he had some wise old comment he wanted to make to me—about perseverance or skill, perhaps even a fawning compliment to make me feel even more puffed up with myself—and then I touched his tail with the tip of my rod and he wavered off into the dark water below the bend and disappeared.

I breathed deeply and smiled and decided that the fish had been a rather nice old evil fellow after all, capable—with his sorcery—of changing a quivering pig's ear into a smug hero. Except for a touch of a shake, probably from the cold, I felt very calm and content.

There was still an hour or more to fish, and then I could fish in the afternoon and evening if I chose, but I clipped off the little mashed fly, wound my line in all the way onto the reel, and disjointed my rod.

When I looked up I saw that a couple of fish had started to rise again in the pool. One of them looked pretty good. I watched them for a few moments and then headed downriver.

Still more time has passed. I am not in the headwaters of Spring Creek but at my desk in a great gray city in the belly of winter. This year I will turn sixty and I have been thinking of time more than I like to admit, and of Camus's observation that at fifty each of us has the face he deserves.

Which face, I wonder—looking at the bewildered but lived-in face in the mirror—is that?

"He is some twenty sev'ral men at least
Each sev'ral hour,"

says George Herbert in "Giddiness," and I still find each of them in me, and other men, too. One of those twenty-odd men fishes—and still feels strange saying *Paraleptophlebia* among strangers. He fishes with a fly rod, mostly for trout, almost always, these days, with a fly that floats. All that seems a minor commitment in a world randomly destructuring itself. I don't know why this old fellow still loves to fish as much as he did when he was six and gigged his first trout on a Carlisle hook strapped to a willow branch, from a mountain brook, or, when at a grim boarding school, he was saved by fishing a sump called

Ice Pond. But he does fish, and some new form of that particular life was defined and hammered into some permanence during those thirty-one days some years ago.

I find it quite wonderful, amid all the ambiguities and tensions of cities and business and the mystery of me, to have a sure and certain thing, like a spring creek, even in my mind, that never fails to bring such fun and serenity, that has filled my head with such indelible images: mornings in the Suburban at the South End Pool, waiting for the first flies to appear; Herb, working his magic and witchery, making impossible casts, long floats; Doug—fifty trout pocking the surface of the flat pool—in extremis; Gillian fishing hard in the freezing rain; McClane, now dead, upright in tropical clothes, nailing some big ones from the fast run; the smell of mint at The Fish Trap; apocalypse at the Paranoid—and apple trees; Herb trying to get the backing onto his reel, his great fish almost in, beaten, then gone; dreaming at the Second Bend Pool and in the headwaters; slapping grasshoppers against the West Branch bends; that great trout feeding in midwater as I stand on the cliff—the fish altogether catchable, *that once*; the sight of Mari as I come down the East Branch, close to her easel, then stepping back, pursuing some thing that might lead far; and my eye following a faint golden spot among other faint golden spots, far out on the pond, inching toward a spreading circle on a grizzly day, coming closer, and then, with a delicate rise, we're hooked.

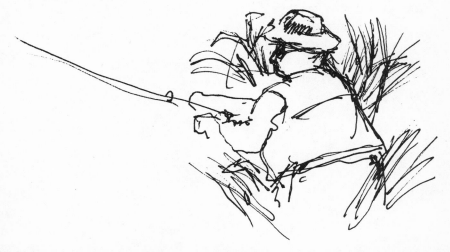